THE HEALING TRADITIONS &
SPIRITUAL PRACTICES OF WICCA

the
Healing Traditions & Spiritual Practices *of* Wicca

DEBBIE MICHAUD

KEATS PUBLISHING

LOS ANGELES

NTC/Contemporary Publishing Group

Library of Congress Cataloging-in-Publication Data is available.

Published by Keats Publishing
A division of NTC/Contemporary Publishing Group, Inc.
4255 West Touhy Avenue, Lincolnwood, Illinois 60646-1975 U.S.A.

Copyright © 2000 by Debbie Michaud.

Design by Laurie Young

Printed in the United States of America

International Standard Book Number: 0-658-00386-0

00 01 02 03 04 VP 18 17 16 15 14 13 12 11 10 9 8 7 6 5 4 3 2 1

To my parents, Alice and Gerry Michaud,
who let their children fly with open minds.

To my husband, Dennis,
who did not complain when I took over the computer.

To my coworkers for their encouragement in this project.

And to Keats Publishing for this grand opportunity.

CONTENTS

1

What Is Wicca?

Wicca is first and foremost a religion—a religion based in a respect of nature. This religion stresses living in harmony with all creatures and the earth. It honors a Goddess and a God, who are contained in all nature and in ourselves. The Goddess and God are an aid for Wiccans—also known as witches—to focus inner power and the power that is found in all of nature, and are seen in many aspects and known by many names. Wiccans believe that the Divine is in us, not just around us or watching from somewhere above us. Wicca is practiced in a group (known as a coven or grove) or alone (as a solitary).

Other names for this recognized religion include Modern Witchcraft, the Craft of the Wise, or the Craft, but the most common name for the religion is Wicca. There has been debate on the origin of the word *Wicca*. It is said to be from the Old

English words *wicce* and *wicca*. Many say these words are from the root *wit*, meaning "wisdom." Others say the Indo-European roots *wic* and *weik*, meaning "to bend or turn," are the basis for the term. The word *wicca* (pronounced wick-kah) is an Anglo-Saxon word meaning "wise," and is actually the masculine form of the word. It is also used in the feminine form *wicce* (pronounced wick-kay), particularly by feminist followers. The plural form is *wiccan*. The word *Wicca* may also be a corruption of the Anglo-Saxon word *witga*, meaning "seer or diviner." To add to the confusion, there is also the Middle English word *wicche*, meaning witch or wizard, that is used both for the masculine and feminine.

Wicca is based in pre-Christian European folklore and mythology, but is heavily influenced by modern texts by writers such as James Frazer and Jules Michelet. Wicca attempts to connect to the Mother Goddess (Mother Earth, Mother Nature) in her aspects of Maiden, Mother, and Crone. Although it is not a prehistoric religion, some of its central ideas are based in the Paleolithic Age when, according to anthropologists, a god of hunting and a goddess of fertility were worshiped. The power of nature inspired ancient people's belief in higher powers that controlled rain, winds, thunder, fire, and the like. And then there was the biological power of women as the givers of life—magickal creatures, indeed.

Individuality, personal spiritual growth, and creativity are encouraged in the Wiccan community. To be Wiccan is to respect all creatures that inhabit this earth with us, and to do our best to live in harmony with them. Wicca is a celebration of life. It is being able to see the wonder of a bird in flight, the way a tree creates new leaves each year, the growth of a flower from a tiny seed. A celebration of the wonders and beauty of this planet we are on, and a concern to preserve it—that is Wicca. It is a journey of appreciation, and dedication to learning.

> Interest in Wicca as a religion was driven to the forefront of popular culture by feminists and others interested in the women's spirituality movement of the 1960s and '70s. Writers such as Z Budapest and Starhawk have shown women a religion that is not controlled by men and have been embraced by the feminist community.

3

COMMON MISCONCEPTIONS ABOUT WICCA

1. Wicca is not a surviving ancient pagan religion of western Europe. It is a modern religion, constructed in the twentieth century by using texts from the period of the Inquisition as well as more modern writings from the late 1880s to the 1930s.

2. Wiccans are not Satanists! Confusion exists because some terms, such as *coven* and *sabbat,* are used in both Wicca and Satanism. Both groups have drawn ideas and terms from the Christian texts of the Inquisition and other works, but they are vastly different.

3. A male witch is not a warlock. *Warlock* is a Scottish word meaning "oath breaker" that first came into vogue after the Inquisition, and then enjoyed a revival in Hollywood movies. Male or female, it does not matter—both are witches.

4. Not all witches wear black. An object appears a certain color because it absorbs all other colors of light except for the color that we see, which it reflects. If we were to mix all the reflected colors, the result would be black. Because of its absorbent, receptive nature, black is a favorite color to use in ritual and is said to be receptive to psychic energy. But during holidays, Wiccans often wear other appropriate colors. For instance, if we are celebrating spring, a green robe is a good choice; and a rich brown works for autumn. Not all of us cover ourselves with jewelry decorated with pentagrams, either.

5. Hollywood has always been guilty of depicting witches as cackling, ugly old women mixing poisonous brews in steaming cauldrons. In recent years, witches have been portrayed as troubled teens solving their problems with dark rituals. The entertainment industry has consistently shown witches in a negative light, and people assume that is the reality. We are nothing like that (although many teens are drawn to Wicca). Film and television depictions of witches place too much emphasis on spells, and little on spirituality.

> A witch may wear a pentagram with the single point up or the single point down. Some traditions have different levels of initiation and wearing the point down will indicate that an individual has "graduated" to a higher level. Satanists always wear the pentagram with the single point down.

NEO-PAGANS: WICCANS ARE PAGANS, BUT NOT ALL PAGANS ARE WICCAN

Wicca is a pagan religion, but not all pagans are Wiccan. Paganism is polytheistic, which refers to pagans' belief in more than one god, including goddesses. Wiccans may choose to work with any of the many gods and goddesses of the world's cultures. According to Jungian theory, the goddesses and gods represent archetypes, or prototypes, that spring from deep within our psyche. These archetypes allow us to explore different parts of our personality and are a way to acknowledge different choices we have to make in life. There are gods and goddesses of strength and of love, of healing and of protection. Pagan pantheons, or groups of goddesses and gods, have many origins; Greek, Roman, Egyptian, and Native American pantheons are arguably the most readily identifiable by the popular culture.

The word *pagan* is from the Latin *paganus*, meaning "country dweller." The negative associations of this word come from centuries of political struggles during which Christianity sought

5

to supersede the older, polytheistic religions of the country people. "Pagan" was used as an insult, much like our modern "hick," and was a derogatory term in Rome by the third century.

Many people continue to think "inferior" when they hear the word pagan, largely because writers in various academic disciplines have depicted tribal religions as inferior and superstitious. Because of a biased, misguided view that all religions developed monotheism in a linear evolution (i.e., that they started as pagan and grew enlightened to monotheism), polytheistic religions became seen as "less evolved." It is now known that there are tribal religions that are monotheistic and have always been so. Nonetheless, to the Christian world, *pagan* continues to mean "irreligious" and "uncivilized." This connotation is deeply embedded in our culture and will be hard to overcome.

Neo-Paganism—a group of modern earth religions derived from Druidry, Shamanism, Goddess spirituality, and contemporary Wicca—is growing in popularity. These systems share some main characteristics: They are polytheistic; they see the world and all things in it as manifestations of the Divine; and they give recognition to female divinity. They take the view that if all is sacred, you should take in life only what you need and replace what you take. In Neo-Paganism, women have a spiritual path that is not restricted or unduly influenced by men. Menstruation and childbirth are celebrated as a sign of the Divine in all women, a perspective that many modern women find refreshing and sadly absent in more mainstream religions.

In Neo-Paganism, you will find a fundamental spiritual need to feel one with the Divine, and that need is met by looking inside yourself. Neo-Paganism also emphasizes the value of rituals.

> There is a theory that in ancient times all women menstruated at the same time—the time of the full moon. It is said that the moon has a powerful influence on the body. Menstrual cycles average twenty-eight days, following the lunar cycle rather than the calendar month. Women who live or work together will often start their period at about the same time.

WICCA OR WITCHCRAFT? WICCAN OR WITCH?

The answer to this question depends on whom you ask. Because Wicca is a modern religion (albeit with some of its foundation in Stone Age beliefs), it has not been passed from generation to generation the way some religions have. Nevertheless, some witches claim to have knowledge of ancestors passed down through generations. This has led to the occasional attitude from witches who claim that "older is better" and Wiccans are not "true witches." The truth is that neither is better nor worse than the other. Both see a connection to all life. Both Wiccans and hereditary witches delight in the energies around us.

To confuse the matter even more, there are families who are practitioners of folk magick who do consider themselves witches. These families do not follow a religious path that is considered Wiccan, nor do they consider the Craft a religion, but they do call themselves witches.

Whether you call yourself "Witch" or "Wiccan" is up to you. Some are more comfortable with one, some with the other. Some people describe themselves as witches as a way to connect with the victims of the Inquisition, a way to connect with the past. No doubt, *witch* has been used for its shock value by some, especially teenagers. (I get so many questions from kids who want to know about spells but who do not care about the spiritual side of the Craft!)

You will find Wiccans come from every socioeconomic and ethnic background you can imagine. And you may be surprised to find that many are professional people: doctors, nurses, lawyers, police officers, business executives. Folks from all walks of life are drawn to Wiccan spirituality, ritual, and tradition.

8

Belief in evil predates the time of the European witch trials, or "witch craze" (1300–1500 A.D.) It was thought that there were several levels of evil. Minor troubles around the home, such as the souring of milk, insects in stored meat, and a bad batch of bread were attributed to fairies, or "little folk." Disease, of humans and animals, was higher up the ladder of evil forces, as was the failure of crops. These problems required the help of "cunning folk," individuals with special knowledge of herbs and/or incantations.

TRADITIONS

There are three major traditions, known as trads, found in the Craft: Gardnarian, Alexandrian, and British Traditional. They are all British in origin. There are other traditions, as well, that integrate concepts from Greek, Celtic, Roman, and Egyptian folklore, to name but a few.

> There is also a secretive side of Wicca. It is inaccessible to most. Some traditions have degrees of initiation. At each degree, more "mysteries" are revealed to the initiates. Structured rituals are performed using images, forms, and languages in a religious, magickal, and mystery context.

Gardnarian

The Gardnarian tradition was founded by Gerald Gardner in England in the 1950s. He is credited with the revival of the Craft. After the repeal of the Witchcraft Act in England in 1951, there was a resurgence of interest in what came to be known as "The Old Ways." Gardner claimed he was initiated into a coven by an hereditary witch with a lineage that was unbroken, but it is now known that the works of Charles Godfrey Leland, Margaret Murray, Rudyard Kipling, Ovid, Aleister Crowley, and Doreen Valiente, among others, form the basic components of

Gardner's rituals. They were not handed down from an old coven. Valiente was a major force in rewriting rituals and bringing the Goddess into the Craft. Gardner's rituals and structure were drawn from Celtic Druidry and the mysteries of Freemasonry, the Key of Solomon, and The Hermetic Order of the Golden Dawn. Gardner combined ideas and rituals from all of these sources, and mixed in a little folk magick.

Alexandrian

The Alexandrian tradition was founded by Englishman Alex Saunders in the 1960s. He called himself the "king of the Witches." It is an offshoot of sorts of the Gardnarian trad, as most of the rituals were copied and adapted from the Gardnarians.

British Traditional

This trad has a base comprised of a mix of Gardnarian and Celtic beliefs. Most British Traditionals have beliefs based on the studies of Janet and Stewart Farrar, the authors of many books (and now videos) on the Craft.

Celtic Wicca

A tradition with a mix of Druid and Celtic concepts, Celtic Wicca stresses the connection to all creatures. Celtic Wiccans know and respect the healing properties of plants and stones. They are also quite aware of the Elemental spirits, such as fairies.

Ceremonial Witchcraft

Ceremonial witches are very formal (and sometimes overly theatrical) in their presentation of rituals. Egyptian magic is a favorite among this group. They are mostly concerned with the magickal aspects of the Craft.

Dianic Tradition

The main focus of the Dianic tradition is the Goddess. Diana's Roman name is Artemis. She was a triple goddess figure of Virgin, Mother, and huntress. She is also known by the names Dione and Diana Nemorensis, Goddess of the Moon. She is the patron saint of childbirth with the name Diana Egeria. During the Inquisition, witches were said to have flown to meet her in the woods. Diana was later to become Madonna, the Mother of Christian cosmology.

The Dianic tradition has been called the "feminist tradition." Followers of the Dianic tradition have been criticized for a lack of balance, as they practice without the God influence. Followers seek to regain the self from male oppression. The Dianic name comes from Margaret Murray's description of the Craft as "the Dianic cult" in her work *Witch-Cult in Western Europe*. This worshiping of goddesses only now draws from Starhawk, Z Budapest, Mary Daly, Merlin Stone, and Barbara Walker, among others.

Hereditary

This group is also known as the family tradition. In order to be considered an hereditary witch, you have to be able to trace the Craft in your family and had to be taught by a relative.

Kitchen Witch

The kitchen has always been a magickal place, and this is the Kitchen Witch's turf. Need a recipe with special "oomph" to it? To a kitchen witch, the tools of cooking are her tools in crafting. No need for any special tools here; her tools are already in the kitchen. Recipes made with love and other intentions can be quite powerful.

Strega

Italian in origin, Strega is associated with a woman known as Aradia in the 1350s.

American writer and folklorist Charles Godfrey Leland's book, *Aradia*, is primarily used in the Strega tradition today. It contains what appears to be the original version of the "Charge of the Goddess." Doreen Valiente, a prominent witch living in England, wrote a version of the Charge for the Gardnarian tradition. This charge has been incorporated into other traditions as well. Valiente's version has been translated by other witches around the world.

Solitary

Also known as solos, or hedge witches, in England, many are following this path. When practicing in the solo tradition, one need not deal with power struggles or hierarchies within one's coven. However, study may be more difficult and good information hard to find.

Solitary practice has soared in popularity since the 1980s. Many have found that it is almost impossible to find a coven willing to take more people. With the broadening acceptance of Wicca as a religion, groups are finding themselves overwhelmed with applicants.

Many books have been released on the Solitary tradition and can be quite helpful to someone starting out.

Eclectic Solitary Witch

This is the person that takes a little from one trad, a little from another, and puts it all together in a way that works for him or her. Is this legitimate? Of course. Not everyone has access to a coven or wants to work with one. The beauty of eclectic solitary is that one works with what is comfortable. It is also more work: You have to do the research and study on your own. Even though it is a legitimate spiritual path, there does sometimes exist a snobbish attitude on the part of those who practice other traditions. They frown on the absence of an initiation into a tradition.

BASIC IDEOLOGY

Principles of Belief

In the fall of 1973, a meeting of witches was held in Minneapolis, Minnesota. The goal of this meeting was to find a modern definition of the word *witch* that would be accepted by the various traditions. The seventy-four attendants of this meeting formed the Council of American Witches in 1974.

These are the principles as set by this council. It was originally printed in *Touchstone*, the newsletter of the Council. They disbanded shortly thereafter.

1. We practice rites to attune ourselves with the natural rhythm of life forces marked by the phases of the Moon and the seasonal quarters and cross-quarters.

2. We recognize that our intelligence gives us a unique responsibility toward our environment. We seek to live in harmony with Nature, in ecological balance offering fulfillment to life and consciousness within an evolutionary concept.

3. We acknowledge a depth of power far greater than is apparent to the average person. Because it is far greater than ordinary, it is sometimes called "supernatural," but we see it as lying within that which is naturally potential to all.

4. We conceive of the Creative Power in the Universe as manifesting through polarity—as masculine and feminine—and that this same Creative Power lives in all people, and functions through the interaction of the masculine and feminine. We value neither above the other, knowing each to be supportive of the other. We value sexuality as pleasure, as the symbol and embodiment of Life, and as one of the sources of energies used in magickal practice and religious worship.

5. We recognize both outer worlds and inner, or psychological, worlds—sometimes known as the Spiritual World, the Collective Unconscious, the Inner

14

Planes, etc.—and we see in the interaction of these two dimensions the basis for paranormal phenomena and magickal exercises. We neglect neither dimension for the other, seeing both as necessary for our fulfillment.

6. We do not recognize any authoritarian hierarchy, but do honor those who teach, respect those who share their greater knowledge and wisdom, and acknowledge those who have courageously given of themselves in leadership.

7. We see religion, magick, and wisdom-in-living as being united in the way one views the world and lives within it—a world view and philosophy of life, which we identify as Witchcraft or the Wiccan Way.

8. Calling oneself "Witch" does not make a Witch—but neither does heredity itself, or the collecting of titles, degrees, and initiations. A Witch seeks to control the forces within him/herself that make life possible in order to live wisely and well, without harm to others, and in harmony with Nature.

9. We acknowledge that it is the affirmation and fulfillment of life, in a continuation of evolution and development of consciousness, that gives meaning to the Universe we know, and to our personal role within it.

10. Our only animosity toward Christianity, or toward any other religion or philosophy-of-life, is to the extent that its institutions have claimed to be "the one true right and only way" and have sought to deny freedom to others and to suppress other ways of religious practices and belief.

11. As American Witches, we are not threatened by debates on the history of the Craft, the origins of various terms, the legitimacy of various aspects of different traditions. We are concerned with our present, and our future.

12. We do not accept the concept of "absolute evil," nor do we worship any entity known as "Satan" or "the Devil" as defined by Christian Tradition. We do not seek power through the suffering of others, nor do we accept the concept that personal benefits can only be derived by denial to another.

13. We work within Nature for that which is contributory to our health and well-being.

16

Wiccan Rede

Wiccans adhere to what is known as the Wiccan Rede, or Rule of Three. This short poem describes the simple Rule of Three: whatever energy you send out, for good or bad, will return to you three times as strong.

> Bide the Wiccan Law ye must,
> In perfect love, in perfect trust.
> Eight words the Wiccan Rede fulfil:
> An ye harm none, do what ye will.
> Ever mind the rule of three:
> What ye sends out, comes back to thee.
> Follow this with mind and heart,
> And merry ye meet, and merry ye part.

This Rede is followed by many traditions. It describes the ideal of love and trust, especially necessary in coven work.

Other than these simple ideals and principles, there is no one belief system in Wicca. There are no dogmas, just a belief in the Goddess and God in and around us. There is no codified quest to find salvation in this world or the next. The lack of dogma seems to attract people who are disillusioned with the Catholic Church and its structure. Each tradition and/or coven constructs its own rules of conduct.

2

The Goddess and the God

Everything in nature has a life force, from the creatures who walk with us on this planet, to the trees and inanimate rocks in the landscape. This concept is known as animism. We are all surrounded by creatures and creations that are divine and sacred.

But in traditional monotheism, divinity has been removed from nature. In Christianity, Judaism, and Islam—all monotheistic religions—divinity resides in one male god, who exploits nature with dominion over all. The Goddess's role as creator was taken over by a male god.

The Goddess is now returning, showing us how to walk carefully upon this earth. With her consort, the God, this sacred couple form the perfect union of opposites, complementing one another.

In Wicca, the Goddess is seen as the creator of all that is. She represents the power of the feminine, and a way to connect to all life on this planet. The women's spirituality movement has embraced the image of the Goddess as a symbol of strength for abused women, a way to nurture self-acceptance and self-esteem, and a model for all women.

The religion of the Goddess has been called both poly-theistic and monotheistic. Goddess worship is polytheistic, in that she has many names and forms. It is also monotheistic, in that all names and forms are symbols of the single Great Mother, the Creator of All. Joseph Campbell, the historian and mytholo-gist, calls this syncretism.

Ancient European pantheons are dominated by the Goddess. She is the creator of the universe, generator of all life. All agricultural societies appear to have worshiped a goddess at one point. In the earliest known creation stories, the Goddess, Mother Nature, call her what you wish, is said to be the source of all being. The Goddess is associated with the female principles of intuition, cyclical nature, nurturing, and all functions of the right brain.

The Goddess surrounds us, to be found in the earth, moon, and stars. She is found in the ebb and flow of the tides, in the bud of a flower. She is found in the creatures of the world. The Goddess is found inside us all, and particularly in women. The bodies of women are sacred and holy, not the things of revulsion that the patriarchal religions would have us believe. If the Goddess is inside us and all that surrounds us, shouldn't we treat all lives as sacred, including our own?

Despite her omnipresence, the Goddess is a mystery never to be fully known.

In the countless myths of the Goddess around the world, one finds some common animal representations—particularly, a preponderance of bird and snake images. Many Goddesses are pictured with egg-shaped bodies and long, birdlike necks. Snakes and birds represent the earth and sky, and both lay eggs. Eggs, symbols of creation, appear in many Goddess myths.

THE TRINITY OF THE GODDESS

The Goddess is manifest in her triple aspects of Maiden, Mother, and Crone. This trinity can be used as a device to understand and acknowledge the three major stages of human life: youth, parenthood, and maturity.

The three aspects of Maiden, Mother, and Crone can also be seen in the three phases of the moon: waxing, full, and waning. Likewise, the cycle of the goddess is seen in the cycles of the harvest: the fallow field, the planted and growing crops, then the harvest itself.

The number three is considered sacred in many goddess cultures, as it is in paternalistic cultures as well. Throughout history, religions have borrowed ideas to add to their own cosmologies. As an example, the Christian Holy Trinity of Father, Son, and the Holy Ghost is adapted from the Hindu trinity of Brahma, Vishnu, and Shiva.

According to Hindu theologians, the Goddess is represented by Yogini, Matri, and Dakini. These three types of priestess typify the trinity of Maiden, Mother, and Crone. These aspects of the Goddess were called deities of nature. Dakini were Tantric priestesses. Their name means "skywalker" and, representing the Crone aspect, the Dakinis were the bringers of death, and attended the dying.

The Maiden

The Goddess in her Maiden aspect symbolizes youth and anticipation of life, the continuation of life, spring, and the waxing moon. The Maiden is associated with the colors white, light pink, and light yellow. In the aspect of the Maiden, we see the world with childlike wonder, with awe at the beauty of a feather and the mystery of a seed. We are eager to start our journey. We also see the Maiden as huntress and warrior, like Athena and Artemis of the classic Greek pantheon. The Maiden is associated with purity and nature, and is usually depicted in the company of animals.

The Mother

The Mother symbolizes summer, ripening, re-creation of life, the high point of the cycle, adulthood and parenthood, and the full moon. The colors associated with the Mother are red (the color of blood and the life force) and green (the color of fertility). In the aspect of the Mother, we learn to take responsibility for ourselves. In ancient societies, the pregnant Mother was a metaphor for the fertile fields that sustained the people of the land. There are a great number of Mother goddesses represented in the world.

The menstrual blood of the Mother has been associated with magick and ritual since Paleolithic times. The blood shed by women was thought to have power for healing and fertility. The mineral oxide red ocher was used to stain images, icons, and even corpses as a symbol of this blood. Paleolithic men reportedly performed surgical procedures on themselves, such as circumcision, in attempt to imitate the bleeding of women for ritual purposes.

23

The Crone

The Crone symbolizes death and the end of cycles, winter, night, menopause, age, wisdom, counsel, and the waning moon. The colors most associated with the Crone are black, dark purple, and gray. The Crone is the way to death and reincarnation. In the aspect of the Crone, we understand that death is a part of life rather than something to be feared. The destructiveness and death in nature is respected, is an aspect of the Goddess called chtonic (meaning earthy), and is part of the Crone. The Crone has the wisdom of many years behind her. In many cultures, the older woman was responsible for the preparation of the dead. The Crone is past menopause; she has the mystery of time behind her. She is the teacher of the secret and the hidden. The onset of menopause, known as the time of Croning, is not to be feared; it is part of the never-ending cycle of the world we live in. The name Crone is not to be feared; it demands understanding and respect.

THE ROLE OF THE GOD

In Wicca, the Goddess and the God are seen as equals; neither can exist without the other. Female and male are both needed for true creation: visualize, if you will, the Great Mother giving life and giving birth to the world, with the God by her side, at times part human, part spirit, part animal. The Goddess and the God each contain a bit of each other, and neither is complete without the partner. They complement each other and are necessary for proper balance.

The God is usually seen as the lover, consort, and son of the Goddess. Like the Goddess, the God also has many names and associations. There is the God as lover, warrior, and the Horned God of the forests. And there is the God of the mysterious Underworld.

Before humans understood the biology of procreation, pregnancy was thought to be caused by ancestral spirits or the light of the moon. When humans better understood themselves, the God was seen as a life force, an impregnator, and hunter. He has been depicted in art as part animal, with horns of a deer or goat and erect phallus. He is also seen as the "Green Man," lord of the forests.

The masculine principle is logical, analytical, and linear. All these qualities are functions of the left brain. The power of the God is called upon when help in logic and analysis is wanted.

He is also associated with the sun and animals. His association with the sun brings the greening of the harvest. He is the harvest, the animals of the forest, the hunter of those animals when necessary, and the ruler of the woods and mountains. He is the lord of light and represents all that is vital. A woman may call upon the God when she feels she needs the strength and assertiveness that he may bring to her.

Why does Wicca recognize so many goddesses and gods? It is because each brings a different strength or attribute to help us live rich lives. When we work with a goddess we have her power to draw on. For example, if a Wiccan is working on a project that involves creativity (say, writing a book), she may draw upon Athena and Hera, goddesses of the Greek pantheon. Athena will bring creativity and assertiveness, Hera her motivation in new endeavors. Some Wiccans draw upon the energy of the Goddess by tapping into the power of nature. The goddesses and gods can be seen as real beings or as archetypes (prototypes). We all have, in our very nature, the power of all the goddesses and gods of the world, and that is the power to conjure and create. We just have to learn to access that power. Drawing from the diverse pool of the gods and goddesses may help us appreciate the diversity of creation and express our full potential.

Myths of the creation and the Goddess and God abound in this world, but there are common threads that run through all of them. The God, representing the sun, dies each year, only to be reborn in the spring. The stories of the Goddess and God are cyclical, as are the seasons of the year. Spring, summer, autumn, and winter can be seen in these stories. Birth, death, and rebirth are the lessons to be learned. All that dies will return with the sun. The eight holidays of the Wheel of the Year are derived from the Creation myths. As we shall see, the Wheel will turn.

THE WHEEL OF THE YEAR

Many earth-based religions such as Wicca use the circle as a description of the cyclical nature of the world. Wicca uses the phrase "Wheel of the Year" to describe this circle. There are many forms of this circle, including the Wheel of the Seasons, the Wheel of the Day, and the Wheel of the Elements. All use the circle, the symbol of the interconnectedness of all things of this world.

A Creation Myth

In the beginning there was She. She was All and All was She. She was the Creator. She was alone and wanted to be so no longer. She, the Mother of All, created life out of herself. She created Him.

He was born to Her and grew strong. She, the Creator, recovered easily from the birth and also grew strong.

He who came from the Mother of All was maturing.

He who was Her Son became her Lover and Consort. She became with child.

He who was Her Consort reached the peak of his power.

He who was her Lover grew older.

His time was over and He who was Her Son and Consort died.

She who was the Creator was again alone. But She was with Child and He who was Her Son would be born again.

And the circle continues. . . .

This is the Wheel of the Year. This never-ending circle marks the changing of the seasons and the travels of the sun. The events on this calendar are rooted in the solar and lunar celebrations of the Celts.

Sabbats

The Craft holidays of the Wheel of the Year are associated with a sun deity, and are called sabbats. Sabbats are the eight standard holidays that are celebrated by most pagans each year. They represent the natural cycle of birth, death, and rebirth. During the Inquisition, witches allegedly held four "Great Sabbats" that were said to be derived from Church festivals, but it is actually the other way around—the Church originally copied the pagan festivals of Candlemas, May Eve, Lammas, and Halloween.

There is little consensus over the origin of the word *sabbat*. Some think the word had a meaning similar to Sunday, the Christian day of rest. The Jewish Sabbath is on Saturday, the seventh day, and is holy. It is also a day of rest. The word *Sabbath* is said to be from *Shabbathai*, the planet Saturn, ruler of the seventh day, a day for rest.

But the word *sabbat* predates Christianity and Judaism, and therefore can have no connection to the Jewish Sabbath. It may be derived from Moorish *zabat*, meaning an occasion of power, or from the Greek *sabatu*, meaning to rest.

The word *sabbat* may also be derived from an alternative name of the god Dionysus: Sabadius or Sabazius. He was worshiped with wild dancing and general all-around raucousness.

During the Inquisition, many old accounts state that there was no salt at the sabbat feasts. Christians of the time claimed that salt was a symbol of salvation and that therefore witches hated it. But according to a recent interpretation by Doreen Valiente, it was the saltcellar, or container, that was missing, not the salt itself. The saltcellar was a mark of social distinction, and there were no such class distinctions at a sabbat. All those attending were considered equals.

> Not all Wiccans celebrate all eight holidays of the Wheel of the Year. Some coven traditions or solitary practitioners prefer to celebrate what are known as the "Greater Sabbats." These are Samhain, Imbolc, Beltane, and Lughnasadh. Whatever your preference on which holidays to celebrate, these holidays keep us in touch with the seasons of this world.

Yule: Winter Solstice, about December 21

It is a time of celebration of the return journey of the sun. The god is born.

Yule is also known as a Quarter. Imagine the year as an unbroken circle—the Wheel of the Year. Divide this circle into four parts, or quarters. The holidays that fall on these points in the Wheel of the Year are Quarters. Yule is one such holiday.

The name *Yule* is said to be from the Old English word *geol*. This was the name of a German pagan midwinter festival. Traditional decorations for the holiday are holly, pine, mistletoe, fruits, and nuts. The wreath, the symbol of the Wheel of the Year, is also quite popular.

Yule is a celebration of fire. Candles are lit as a way to entice the sun to return. The traditional Yule log is the symbol of the coming of the newborn sun. Yule is considered the end of the solar year, as it has the longest night and shortest day of the year.

Imbolc: February 2

The sun is getting stronger. The warmth feels wonderful after the long, cold nights of winter. The promise of spring can be felt in that warmth. It is a time of creativity and inspiration. Imbolc is also known as a Cross Quarter. Imagine the Wheel of the Year divided into eighths; the Cross Quarters are the holidays that fall on these points.

In the United States, February 2 is known as Groundhog Day. German settlers in North America in the 1700s brought the tradition of the Christian Candlemas Day (Imbolc) with them. It was said that if the weather was fair on that day, the rest of winter would be cold and stormy. In Germany they would have searched for a badger. Badgers were used as a signal of spring since their activities increase in early February. Because settlers found no European-type badgers in the United States, they kept an eye out for the groundhog instead.

The traditions of the holiday tell of the making of the corn doll or "Corn Bride." The doll was made of corn or grain and constructed of either the first or the last sheaves of the year's crop. Other decorations include St. Bridget's Cross, an equilateral cross made of grain, and candles.

The Corn Bride represents the harvest, and has many names from many places. Some know her as Corn Mother, Harvest Mother, and Old Wife.

Imbolc is a festival of lights and candles are set all around.

Ostara: Spring Equinox, about March 21

This is the first day of spring. It is a time of starting anew, and of warmth and light. Ostara is a Quarter.

The word is derived from the German goddess of fertility Ostera, also known as Eostre. The origins of Easter are found with this goddess—if the church could not eliminate a pagan celebration it would incorporate it into a celebration of its own.

In the story of Ostera, a rabbit wanted to please her goddess. The rabbit laid some sacred eggs and then decorated them. The eggs were presented to the goddess as a gift. Goddess Ostera was so pleased with the gift she asked the rabbit to share them with the world. The rabbit did as the goddess asked and delivered eggs to everyone. The rabbit and the egg are recognized symbols of fertility and new life.

Beltane: May 1

May is the time of flourishing new growth. It is a time of love. Beltane is a Cross Quarter. It is the beginning of summer when the Goddess and God are Mother and Lover. This sabbat is a fertility celebration: fertility of the crops, animals, new ideas, and the world.

The name is said to be from the Scottish-Gaelic word *beal-tainn*, meaning the "fires of Belos," which refers to bonfires used during the celebration. It is the time of the maypole. A pine tree was originally used for this celebration, and was replaced by the phallic symbol of the pole. Participants dance around the pole intertwining red and white ribbons, the colors of the Goddess and God. Traditional decorations include greenery, flowers, and wreaths of flowers and ribbons.

> The first day of May is also known as May Day. It is one of the pagan festivals the church assimilated because it could not erad-icate it. Radical labor movements in the now-defunct Soviet Union had marked May Day as an important holiday for demonstrations.

Midsummer: Summer Solstice, about June 21

The Summer Solstice is a time of nature's abundance. It is a Quarter. This holiday is celebrated with decorations of flowers, rituals of fire, and blessings for the animals.

It was considered unlucky to marry during the darker months of winter. And because May was sacred to the gods and goddesses, it was forbidden for mortals to marry in this month. So June was the first available month for humans to wed, and became the traditional month for weddings in Ireland and the United States.

Lughnasadh: August 1

As summer is waning, lughnasadh (pronounced loo-na-sa) is reserved as a time of giving thanks for the bounty. This holiday is a Cross Quarter.

The name is said to translate as "assembly of Lugh," in the honor of the Irish God of that name. Lugh is a god of the sun and fertility.

Lughnasadh is the first of three harvest holidays and also marks the weaning of the lambs and calves. The Christian name for this holiday is Lammas, meaning loaf-mass, commemorating the first harvest. It is also known as the Sabbat of the First Fruits. Threshing of the harvest was considered a sacred act and the threshing barn a sacred place. An old fertility custom is still practiced when a new bride is carried over the threshold.

32

Lughnasadh is the time of the sacrifice of the God; his time is waning, and he knows his time here is limited. His energy is in the grain harvested at this time. This is a good holiday on which to treat yourself. Celebrate the harvest by baking a loaf of bread. Make it from scratch if you are able, and share it with a friend.

Mabon: Autumn Equinox, about September 21

The light begins to lessen, and the God is dying. Mabon is a Quarter. It is a continuation of the harvest, when the fields are being cleared of their bounty. Winter is coming. It is a time of balance, the waning sun, and the Harvest Moon. Traditional projects include the making of wine and the gathering of seeds for the next year. Mabon decorations include Indian corn hung on doors, cornstalks in the yard, and pumpkins and gourds on the steps.

Samhain: October 31

Samhain (pronounced sow-en) marks the pagan new year, and is commonly known as Halloween. The veil between the worlds of life and death is thin on this night; we take this time to remember our loved ones who have died. The God gives his life up to the land, and passes into the Shadowland, to be reborn again at Yule. Samhain is a Cross Quarter. It is a time of transition, the time the light half of the year gives way to the dark. Winter is coming.

33

Celebrations for these holidays usually cover three days: the day before, the day of, and the day after the days given as the dates of the holiday.

The dates of the solstices at midsummer and midwinter, and equinoxes in spring and autumn, will vary depending on the Sun's entry into the zodiacal signs of Capricorn for the Winter Solstice, Cancer for the Summer Solstice, Aries for the Spring Equinox, and Libra for the Autumnal Equinox.

The wheel turns again. It is the story of life, death, and rebirth of the God, of the land and the crops, and of ourselves. It is the story of the Goddess and God, and it is the story of our lives. This cycle also demonstrates what can be called the darker side of Wicca (darker *not* being evil). Death always comes; it is inevitable and not always pleasant. But it is as it should be: We are born; we live for a time; and when that time is over, we die. Life is created and destroyed. Death is nothing to fear, it just is.

> If you are not able to take time off from work for these celebrations, take a moment out of the day to recognize the Wheel. During Yule, if you are where it snows, hear the crunch of the snow under your feet as you walk. Really listen to the sound and rejoice in the season. In spring, feel the increasing warmth of the sun. In summer, enjoy the flourishing of the flowers and trees. In autumn, breathe deep the scent of the dropping leaves.

Modern Sabbats

If the celebration is to be outside, there will usually be a fire; try to find a private spot not too far from running water, if possible. The elements of Air and Earth will already present at the site. Celebrations usually include dancing, chanting, making music, food, drink, and magickal workings. Indoor modifications include a smaller fire on an altar (in the form, let's say, of a candle) with the other Elements also represented there.

Esbats

Lunar holidays are also known as esbats, a time of celebrating the full moons. Any Wiccan ritual held at any time other than a Sabbat is also considered an esbat. The word *esbat* is said to be from the French word for "frolic." It is a time of celebration of the different full moons of the year and a time for magick. If you are part of a working coven, it is also a time of social gathering. It is customary to write a different ritual for each of the full moon celebrations.

There is a ritual in the modern Craft called "Drawing Down the Moon," a ritual performed during the full moon. Each coven has a priest and priestess, equals in the coven. The priest invokes the Goddess of the moon into the priestess for the duration of the ritual. Some priestesses may enter a trance state. Others may take the "part" of the Goddess. The energy of the moon and/or the Goddess in the representation of the moon is used in rituals and spells.

Due to the rotation of the earth, there are thirteen full moons in the solar year. A full moon happens every 28¼ days. Full-moon energy is used for banishing unwanted influences, protection, and divination. A full moon is also a good time for planning, releasing, and working backwards in time. Full-moon magic can be done for seven days (starting three days before the full moon and ending three days after).

Each full moon has a traditional name. There are actually many names for each of the full moons, drawn from many cultures, but these seem to be the most popular of the moon names:

January's full moon is known as the Wolf Moon. This is possibly from the *Wolf-Monath* (meaning "Wolf Month"), the beginning of the old Saxon year.

The moon of February is known as the Storm Moon. It is a time of strong weather.

The month of March brings the Chaste Moon, so called possibly because this is the time of the Maiden aspect of the Goddess.

April's full moon is called the Seed Moon. It is the traditional time for starting seeds indoors or outdoors.

May's full moon is known as the Hare Moon. This may be a reference to the myth of the rabbit and the Goddess discussed under the sabbat Ostara.

The moon of June is known as the Dyad Moon. The word *dyad* is from the Greek *duad*, meaning "two." It refers to the myth of the marriage of the Goddess and God during this month.

The month of July brings the Mead Moon. It was a traditional time for the making of mead, a fermented beverage made of water, honey, malt, and yeast—much like our modern ales.

In August comes the Wyrt or Wort Moon. *Wort* is an old Anglo-Saxon word for herb. This is the time for the herbal harvest.

September's full moon is known as the Barley Moon, and also the Harvest Moon. This month was the traditional month for the barley harvest. This is the full moon closest to the Autumnal Equinox.

The month of October brings the Blood Moon, probably a reference to the slaughtering of the farm animals for food at this time, in preparation for the approaching winter.

The full moon of November is called the Snow Moon.

Colder weather is on the way, bringing the snows of winter with it.

December's full moon is known as the Oak Moon. The name refers to the tree that is sacred to the God.

The second full moon in any one calendar month is known as a Blue Moon. This happens, on average, once every two-and-a-half years.

> The word lunatic is from the Latin *luna*, meaning moon. Ancient cultures believed insanity, or lunacy, was caused by the moon. It was thought that the effect was intensified by a full moon. It was considered dangerous to sleep outside under moonlight. Other results of such folly included blindness and swelling of the face.

3

Magick

*M*agick. In Wicca, it is a common practice to add the *k* to the word *magic* to differentiate it from the magic that stage performers do. *Magick* with the *k* came into common usage when Aleister Crowley reintroduced the world to the Ceremonial Magick of the Hermetic Order of the Golden Dawn. Crowley did not follow the Wiccan Rede, but the ways of the Ceremonial Magician. His rule was "Do what thou wilt shall be the whole of the law." Wiccans and witches perform magick, but that does not make anyone who performs magick a witch. There are many forms of magick, and different styles of portraying it. For instance, ceremonial magick is very elaborate and formal, more of the robes-and-props style. Folk magick is usually very simple and utilizes everyday items.

Even Christians practice magick, and have since the founding of the church. Amulets were worn around the neck for protection against evil. One popular amulet sported the many different names of God and was said to keep death away from the wearer. Amulets still exist in the form of the crucifix, and St. Christopher medals. The magick of holy water as a purifier is well recognized.

The word *magic* is said to be from the Middle English word *magik*, meaning an attempt to forecast or control forces of nature. This was done by the use of energy in rituals or spells. The word *magic* may also be from the Greek *mageia* or *magikos*, meaning "arts of the Magi." The arts of the Magi refers to the religion and occult practices of the Magi, the priests of the monotheistic religion known as Parsiism in Persia (about 600 B.C.).

Rituals involve the conjuring of energy by chanting, dancing, and drumming. Energy is raised and directed for the purpose intended. Practicing magick is not a game and the effect you are after takes thought and planning. You need to remember that all your actions will always create a reaction.

Magick is not supernatural, meaning it is not outside the natural world. It is all around us and within us. It is contained in all life on this planet. Magick may also be found in what are usually considered inanimate objects, such as rocks. It is our task, as Wiccans, to get in touch with magickal energy.

In Wicca you will come across the phrase "So mote it be." This is used after the completion of a spell or ritual. The word *mote* is from the Middle English *moten* which is in turn derived from the Old English word *motan*. These words mean "might" or "may." The phrase "So mote it be" is used to enforce the spell.

Magick is not in and of itself good or evil. The use of the magickal energy is up to the user. The Wiccan is bound by the Rede to do no harm, to others or to him- or herself. Magick takes concentration and discipline. With visualization and relaxation, Wiccans gain access to mysterious power of the mind. Often, when practicing magick one will enter a light trance state.

Magick may be a complicated matter or it may be more user-friendly, depending on the practitioner. It can be quite structured as to how and when to do certain things. Magick uses the vibrations and energy carried in all things on the planet, from herbs, trees, and stones, to the energy held in colors.

Many books on magick contain charts on associations of times, moon phases, and so forth. Some of the literature will describe spells that must be performed at a certain moon phase, at a certain time of the year, and at a certain time of the night. It can be intimidating. Magick, to me, is mostly a state of mind. The time does not matter; the intent does.

Not everyone who performs magick is a witch. Ceremonial magick, for instance, is derived from the Hebrew Qabalah.

Ceremonial magicians use nonpagan texts such as the Key of Solomon. They seek to control nature by calling entities—angels or demons—with the intent to assume control of the forces of nature from those entities. This form of magick is very ritualized and theatrical. It has no connection to the pagan gods and goddesses of the witch.

MOON MAGICK:
LUNAR PHASES AND MAGICKAL WORK

Because Wiccans are attuned to the moon's beauty and its association with the Goddess, moon magick is one of the most popular forms of magick. The basics of moon magick are easy to follow.

The energy of the new moon is used for personal growth, healing, and the blessing of a new project. For example, if you are stuck in a rut with your music lessons, perform a ritual on the new moon to help you get to the next level.

Between the new moon and full moon is the phase called the waxing moon. During this phase, the moon emits a more intense light. Magick during this phase includes attraction magick, or love magick. This is the time to make statements on how your life should be. Create spells for abundance, growth, and gain.

Between the full moon and new moon is the phase called the waning moon. During waning, the light of the moon diminishes. Magic for this phase includes banishing magick, such as losing negative emotions, bad habits, and the like. Are you having trouble dealing with bad feelings from a broken relationship? Write a ritual and have them lifted at this time.

Three days before the new moon is the dark moon, named so because the moon is not visible in the sky. Traditionally, no magick is performed at this time. It is a time for rest. Enjoy the mystery and dark of the night sky.

Before the use of a newly purchased crystal ball, you will need to clear, or purify, it. First, soak the ball in a bowl of sea water for twenty-four to forty-eight hours. Remove the ball and give the salt water back to the earth, but be careful not to pour it on any plants. Then put the ball outdoors in a safe place where the light of the moon will touch it. The best time to purify is between the waxing and the full moon.

43

Myths

In premodern times, nature and the changing seasons had a great impact on religious ceremonies. Because the moon was seen as a symbol of the Goddess, its light was considered magickal, and a source of energy. Today, Wiccans often practice magick at a full moon to tap into this energy.

In many cultures, the Moon Goddess and the Creatress were the same. Polynesians called the Creatress Hina, meaning moon. She was the first woman, and every woman is a *wahine*, created in the image of Hina. Scandinavians sometimes called the Creatress Mardoll, translated as "Moon Shining over the Sea."

Ashanti people had a generic term used for all their deities: *Boshun*, meaning "moon." The Sioux call the moon The Old Woman Who Never Dies. The Iroquois call her Eternal One. The rulers in the Eritrean zone of South Africa gave the Goddess the name Moon. The Gaelic name of the Moon, *gealach*, came from *Gala* or *Galata*, the name of the original Moon-Mother of Gaelic and Gaulish tribes. The Moon was called *Metra*, which means "Mother Whose Love Penetrated Everywhere." In the Basque language, the words for *deity* and *moon* are the same. *Menos* meant "Moon" and "power" to the Greeks. To the Romans, the morality of the Moon Goddess was above that of the Sun God.

Gnosticism was an early Christian mystery cult. Gnostics were said to focus on a goddess and practiced Tantric-type meditation, with a special interest in sexual rites. The Gnostic sect of Naasians believed in a primordial being known as "the heavenly horn of the moon." The Moon was thought of as the Great Mother. The Gnostics were said to have knowledge of secrets of the afterlife to ensure their place in heaven.

Not surprisingly, the Orthodox church opposed the Gnostic use of feminine images.

The root word for both "moon" and "mind" is the Indo-European *manas, mana,* or *men*, representing the Great Mother's "wise blood" in women, the flow of which was governed by the moon. The derivative *mania* was used to mean ecstatic revelation, as *lunacy* meant possession by the spirit of Luna, the Moon. To be "moontouched" or "moonstruck" meant to be chosen by the Goddess. When patriarchal thinkers belittled the Goddess, these words came to mean "craziness."

Orphic and Pythagorean sects viewed the moon as the home of the dead, a female gate known as Yoni. Souls passed through on the way to the paradise fields of the stars. Greeks often located the Elysian Fields, home of the blessed dead, in the moon. The shoes of Roman senators were decorated with ivory crescents to show that after death they would inhabit the moon. Roman religion taught that the moon would purify the souls of the honorable. Wearing the crescent was "visual worship" of the Goddess. That was why the prophet Isaiah denounced the wearing of lunar amulets by Zion women.

Because the moon was the holder of souls between reincarnations, it sheltered both the dead and unborn, who were one and the same. If a man dreamt of his own image in the moon, he would become the father of a son. If a woman dreamt of her own image in the moon, she would have a daughter.

45

Ancient alchemists believed the moon to be watery and cold, and thought it might be the origin of dew and rain. The alchemists attempted to collect moonlight in polished silver basins. This may be the source of the superstition that if you turn a silver coin in your pocket at the first sign of the new moon, good luck will follow.

The Moon Goddess created time, with all its cycles of creation: growth, decline, and destruction. This is why ancient calendars were based on phases of the moon and women's related menstrual cycles. The moon still determines agricultural work in some parts of India. Indonesian moon priestesses were responsible for finding the right phase of the moon for every undertaking.

The moon was supposed to rule life and death, as well as the tides. People living on the shores of large bodies of water were convinced that a baby could only be born on an incoming tide and a person could not die until the tide went out. It was often said birth at a full tide or a full moon meant a lucky life. Girls in Scotland refused to wed on anything but a full moon.

During the eclipse of the moon, the Babylonians thought ceremonies and fasting would get them through this time of peril. Western Africans thought the lunar eclipse was a time of bewitching and the possibility of catching a cold was greater. Devils were banished by the people of Bali during these eclipses. Orinoco tribes thought that if the moon was extinguished, the light of the earth would also be extinguished. They buried lighted brands in the earth to keep her safe.

The moon has an elliptical orbit. This means that at times it is further away from the earth than at other times in its orbit. It also rotates on its own axis in the same time period as it revolves around the earth. Because of this, we always see the same face of the moon.

TOOLS OF THE CRAFT

Most religions use tools in their practices. Wicca is no different. Through our touch and intention, energy may be directed through these tools to invoke the Deities or accomplish our goals. These tools are not absolutely necessary and many Wiccans do not have or want all of them. The tools themselves have no power, just as statues and symbols of the Goddess and God do not have power. The power comes from within you.

You need to change your mind-set when doing ritual and magickal work. These tools help you to do that. They are a way to help your mind focus on your intention and to connect to the power of the Goddess and God that is deep within us all.

Although an occult shop is one place to find your tools, it can be a lot of fun to search antique shops, flea markets, fairs, junk shops, and even malls for items you may use. I found my cauldron in the kitchenware section of a department store. Its original use was as a vegetable cooker for outdoor grills. It is made of cast iron, and has the characteristic round shape, wider at the top than at the base. It rests on three legs and has a handle. My little "cooker" is the perfect altar cauldron.

Many Wiccans are craftspersons and choose to make some of their own tools, as well.

The Athame

The athame is a magick knife. It is used not for cutting but to direct energy raised during rituals and spells. It is a double-edged knife that is usually dull, with a black or dark-colored handle.

Black absorbs the energy from you and the area around you. Some Wiccans engrave their athame with magickal symbols (though it is by no means a necessity).

The word *athame* seems to be a derivation of the word *al-dhamme*. A knife by that name was used by Arab-Andalusian-Moorish moon worshipers called "the Double-Horned Ones." The knife was used for ritual scarring.

Some Wiccans, men in particular, like to substitute a sword in place of the athame. It has all the qualities of a knife, but because of its size it is difficult to use indoors without knocking something over. Stories about magickal swords are common in mythic literature, and are usually associated with men and strength.

The magickal symbolism of the knife is change. It is linked with the Element of Fire. Its straight phallic shape links it with the God.

48

The Boline

The boline is a white-handled knife. It is an actual cutting knife. It is used to cut herbs and wands, to inscribe symbols on other magickal items, or to cut cords. It is used not just in the ritual circle used for spell casting (see pages 65–76), but also in everyday life.

The Bell

The bell has long been associated with the mystical. Oriental tradition uses bells as a protection from evil or negative forces. The Christian Church was influenced by the orient and used bells for the same purpose. The arrival of the Holy Spirit was signified by the ringing of a bell. The bell defined times of worship.

Bells were also considered magickal because of their position high in the steeple of a church. In the steeple they were high above the earth but not in heaven. Church bells were also rung during storms to chase demons away. Children were given bells to wear to avert the evil eye.

Like everything else around you, bells carry energy. When a bell is rung, vibrations are released. The effects differ, depending on its tone, its volume, and material from which the bell is made. Any type of bell may be used. It may take some experimenting to find one to your liking.

A bell is usually rung to signal the beginning and the end of a ritual or section of a spell. It also may ward off negativity or evoke good energies. It is considered a protector if hung on a door.

The bell is a feminine symbol. It is often used to invoke the Goddess in ritual.

The Broom

The broom has become a powerful symbol and tool against curses. Even today, many people hang a broom on the front door of their home, but most do not know the symbolism behind the decoration (see below).

The broom is used in ritual and magick. This tool is sacred to both the Goddess and God. The area to be used for ritual is swept clean with the broom. This sweeping is not just a physical sweeping of the premises; one must visualize the broom sweeping out all the negativity in the area. This clears the way for better magick. The broom is a purifier that is linked with the Element of Water, which is also a purifier. It is used in all types of water spells.

History and Lore

Brooms were used in pagan rituals of marriage and birth and have long been associated with witches. In Rome, the broom was a symbol of Hecate's priestesses and midwives, who swept the threshold of a house after each birth to remove evil spirits that might harm the child and the mother.

The broom's stick is traditionally made of ash as a symbol of protection. The stick represents the male. The brush is traditionally made from birch twigs for exorcism, purification, and protection, and represents the female principle. A branch of willow is used to bind the stick and the brush together. The willow represents protection, healing, and love.

The broom is also used to signify sexual union. Jumping over a broom set on the ground was a favorite wedding custom. Medieval peasant weddings were not performed in a church and came under the area of common law. By the time of the Renaissance, the broom was closely identified with nonecclesiastical marriages. When the Catholic church began to take over wedding rites, marriages "by the broom" became illegitimate, and those who did so were considered lacking in morals. Because of the sexual symbolism involved, the word *besom*, or broom, was used as slang to describe a "loose" woman.

Sufi mystics entered Spain in the early Middle Ages. They organized themselves into groups of thirteen, much like covens.

The Sufi sages rode horse-headed canes called *zamalzain*, or "gala limping horse." To the Sufi, the stick horse stood for the Pegasus-like fairy steed that carried him to heaven and back. Customs like this became prevalent among the Basques, and they were frequently accused of witchcraft. You will find modern-day variations of the Sufi stick with the horse's head in toy shops.

Flying

Modern legends of flying are rooted in the witches' use of an ointment that contained aconite. This drug is readily absorbed through the skin and mucous membranes and produces sensations of giddiness, confusion, lethargy, and tingling followed by numbness, and so may have effected the feeling of flying. Pre-Colombian Mexico worshiped a goddess who rode naked on a broom, so this idea is not new to legends.

51

The Censer

Another name for the censer is the thurible. The censer holds the incense burned during ritual. It may be made of fancy metal; it may be a beautiful shell from the sea. Be sure to have a fireproof base on which to rest it, as it can get quite hot. Incense is an important religious symbol; its smoke and fire are used to purify. The scent of incense also affects emotions, and reaches the deep consciousness. It relaxes the mind, preparing it for the working of magick.

There are two types of incense. One type needs charcoal to burn. This incense is made of gum resins or woods. It is crushed, blended, and formed into cubes. The other is the more common stick variety that burns by itself. It is easier to handle, and may be burned in a bowl with sand.

The Cauldron

The word *cauldron* is said to derive from the Latin *cauldus*, meaning "hot," and the Sanskrit *cra*, "to boil."

The word *caudle* also comes from the same Sanskrit root. Caudle is a spiced gruel used for healing. Caudle was fed to women who were confined (i.e., undergoing childbirth) and to those who came to see a new baby at home.

In Britain and Ireland, tales abound with stories of heroic adventures in which the prize was a magick cauldron. (This cauldron image seems to have evolved into a cup.) The Avalon tales of the search for the Holy Grail have their roots in pre-Christian myths. The Grail in the original stories was named "The Cauldron of Inspiration and Rebirth."

The cauldron is an ancient vessel of cooking, full of magickal tradition and mystery. It is often the focal point of rituals. During spring rites, it may be filled with flowers. During winter, you may have a small fire in it to represent the returning heat and light of the sun (the God) from the cauldron (the Goddess). The cauldron may be used for scrying (also known as gazing, or fortune-telling) by filling it with water.

The cauldron should be made of iron and have three legs. These three legs represent the triple aspect of the Moon Goddess. The opening should be wider at the top than at the base. The shape of the cauldron represents Mother Nature, and the three legs the triple face of the Moon Goddess. Cauldrons come in many sizes. This is usually the hardest tool to find, especially if you are looking for a used one; and the cost is high, especially compared with other tools.

The cauldron is a symbol of the Goddess, the essence of femininity and fertility. It is also a symbol of the Element of Water, reincarnation, immortality, and inspiration.

The Cup

You may use a cup made of any material that strikes your fancy. Silver, brass, pottery, stone—anything will work. There are many beautiful cups, also known as chalices, on the market. Just remember, it does not need to be ornate. A simple cup made of pottery will serve you just as well as a crystal one.

The cup is a matriarchal symbol of the womb. In pre-Christian thought, this image evolved into that of a chalice filled with sacrificial blood of humans and animals. Christianity changed the blood to wine, because the sacrifice of humans and animals was considered distasteful.

It is also a symbol of the Goddess and fertility. It is used to hold water, or any beverage to be consumed for ritual.

The Pentagram/Pentacle

A pentagram is a five-point star. There is an early example of this form in Babylon. The Christians likened the five points of the star to the five wounds of Christ on the Cross. The image appeared occasionally in the church architecture. The pentagram is also found in Freemasonry, and the Qabalah is said to be the most probable place of origin.

The followers of Pythagoras called the pentagram "pentalpha," because the shapes of the points formed the letter *A* five times. The pentagram is also called Druids Foot, Wizards Foot, and Goblins' Cross in different parts of Middle Europe.

The pentacle is a flat piece made of brass, gold, silver, wax, clay, wood, or other material that is inscribed with the pentagram. There are many beautiful pentacles for sale, but they can be quite expensive, so a good project would be to make your own out of wood. You will find rounds of wood in your local craft shop. Just have fun inscribing a pentagram on it and embellish it any way you wish. Objects that are to be ritually consecrated are placed upon the pentacle. The pentacle represents the Element of Earth.

In Wicca, four of the five points of the pentagram represent the Elements of Earth, Air, Fire, and Water. The top point represents Spirit, set above all others. It is worn for protection against negativity. In some Wiccan traditions, it is worn with the single point down, as a symbol of the second degree of learning. It is most often worn with the single point up.

The Wand

The word *wand* is derived from the Gothic word *windan*, meaning "wind" or "bind." The wand is used to bind the energy of the spell together.

The wand has been used for thousands of years in religious and magickal rites. The Goddess and God are invoked with the wand. The wand is also used to direct energy, to draw magickal symbols during ritual. Wands may also be used to stir a magickal brew in your cauldron.

The wand represents the Element of Air and evokes the energy of the spell. The energy is sent in the direction the wand is pointing. As with all of these tools, the wand is not absolutely necessary. It is a tool to help focus your mind and energy. Some people enjoy them for the special feeling they give, or for their beauty. Some Wiccans feel no need for wands and use their arms and hands instead. If you do decide to use a wand, however, you may want to construct your own, using metal or wood.

Making a Metal Wand

Go to your local hardware or home-improvement store. Find a length of metal tubing with a diameter that will fit comfortably in your hand. Attach a crystal at one end using leather to wrap the crystal and secure it to the metal. At the other end use fabric, leather, or other material for the grip.

Engrave the wand with runes or symbols of your choice using an etching tool. Decorate your wand with what you feel is appropriate—stones, feathers, shells, and beads can add just the right magickal touch.

Making a Wooden Wand

Take a walk in the woods. Feel the energy of the living trees around you. Be aware of the life and magick in the woods. Listen to the birds, the squirrels, the wind. Touch the trees as you pass them. Listen to the inner voice of life emanating from the bark. When you have found the tree that will give you your wand, you will know. You will feel it is right. There are lists of magickal trees, but you may have to do some research to find what is indigenous to your area.

You may use a fallen branch from this tree, or you may cut the tip off one of the branches. A wand twelve to eighteen inches long is about right. Look for one that is relatively straight and has a comfortable weight and circumference. Thank the tree for its gift by leaving a gift in return—a flower, a shell, a stone, or coin—for the tree and the fairy folk of the woods.

You may remove the bark on the branch, or leave it on. You may decorate your wooden wand any way you choose. Add a crystal to the top and attach it with a leather strap; carve symbols; or add stones, feathers, or beads.

Book of Shadows

Some say the name "Book of Shadows" indicates that the Other World's realities can only be a shadow when written. But it is also referred to as the Book of Illumination and the Book of Light, among other names. It all sounds very mysterious, but it is not, really. It is simply a place to keep notes. It can be anything from a simple journal or a spiral notebook to a fancy leather-bound book. In it is placed everything the Wiccan wants to document: answers to questions, candle and/or moon magick, Witchcraft history, herbal information, spells. You may want to keep separate volumes for different kinds of information.

The Book of Shadows is thought to have more power if it is handwritten. But some Wiccans now have a "Disc of Shadows." The typewritten word is easier to read and people simply type faster than they write. (Others, like myself, have handwriting that is quite dreadful, and so prefer the keyboard!)

Many covens have their own Book of Shadows, and initiates are encouraged to copy from it. Then, as they become more experienced, they are expected to add to it.

Robes

Robes may be worn for ritual or spell work. If celebrating the seasons, choose a robe in the appropriate color. Traditional robes are long sleeved, floor length, and hooded. A cord is worn at the waist.

Candles

Candles have long been used in religious ceremonies. They represent the power of light coming out of the darkness, as well as knowledge and spiritual illumination. Ancient civilizations used fire to symbolize the life force within each of us.

Wiccans use candles to represent the elements, the Goddess and God, and the specific goals of ritual and spell work. Candles are also used to focus thought during meditation and to create a special atmosphere.

You may carve special patterns or runic symbols on your candles, if you wish, although this is not necessary. There are many magickal symbols to choose from, and they can help you achieve the right mind-set.

Use fresh candles that are not cracked for each spell. Let the candles burn down, but *do not* leave the candles unattended.

Place the burning candles in a safe place, away from drafts, and where they will not fall; and always keep an eye on them. Candles left burning on their own have been the cause of many deadly fires. If the spell or ritual calls for the entire candle to be used, light it over several nights; it is safer that way.

Candles may be lit with matches or a lighter. Some Wiccans will object to use of the matches, because of the sulfur they contain. Some will object to the lighter, because it contains petroleum product. Use what makes you most comfortable.

Try to use hand-dipped candles when you can, as they burn slower than factory candles. Beeswax is best as it comes straight from nature and is therefore considered more powerful. (Note that beeswax candles are also more expensive and may be a luxury item that many cannot afford.)

Try to keep at least two candles of each color. You never know when they will be needed. Keep more of the white and black on hand. White candles may be substituted for other colors, and the black may be hard to find—except at Samhain.

THE ALTAR

Your altar is a personal place for ritual and meditation. It is a place where the Divine and the spiritual can be experienced in your home. It is a place where your thoughts and feelings may be expressed in any way you wish.

Your altar does not have to be elaborate. It can be a small table, a mantelpiece, windowsill, a shelf in a bookcase, or whatever else is available in your home. It can be round to represent the Goddess, square, symbolic of the elements, rectangular, or oval. It may be a small area of ground in a field or wood. If you have a sheltered garden, consider getting a beautiful stone bench.

You may decorate your altar with stones, crystals, talismans, herbs, flowers, or (a favorite of mine) feathers. Candles, shells, incense, and representations of animals are popular ornaments, too. You may wish to find an image of the Goddess and God, or an assortment of Goddess and God images, for your altar. They may be changed for different rituals and celebrations. Or, you may have favorite images that you always use. Remember, Wiccans do not worship the images, they are but representations of the power available to us. In short, an altar reflects the personality of the individual who puts it together.

To find items for your altar, take a hike in the woods or a walk on the beach. You will find many treasures along the way. Pick up objects that attract your eyes—a stone, twigs, acorns, leaves, feathers. On the beach you will find shells, bits of dried seaweed, and wood. All these items bring wonderful energy to your altar.

It is considered best to place the altar facing north. This direction symbolizes the power flow from darkness to light and is associated with the Earth. Some choose to face the altar south honoring the Sun as it rises in the east. Different traditions and cultures have different ideas on the placement of altars. You may wish to research these traditions and decide what placement is best for you.

Many rituals and spells call for the use of an altar and the casting of a circle. In this case the altar is usually set in the center of the circle. Again, the direction depends on what tradition, if any, you are following. Any altar you create may be used permanently or taken down after each use.

Altar Setup

The Goddess is associated with the left side of the altar, and may be represented by a white, silver, or green candle. A sculpture or some sort of figure may also be used. Tools that are associated with the Goddess are the cup, pentacle, bell, crystals, and the cauldron. These tools may be set on the left side of the altar or toward the center. If the cauldron is large, it is usually placed on the floor to the left of the altar.

The God is associated with the right side of the altar. A sculpture or a figure of some sort may be used to represent the God. A popular symbol of the God is an acorn, because of the oak's association with the God. A red, yellow, or gold candle is appropriate. Tools associated with the God are the censer, wand, athame, and boline. They are set to the right.

This setup is for a simple ritual involving few tools. It is a good layout for beginners; it has just the very basics and will be less confusing than trying to set up and use a large altar.

Remembering the balance of all, the censer and cauldron are sometimes set in the middle of the altar for offerings to both Goddess and God. The pentacle is sometimes set in front of the censer. It marks the directions and/or elements of the circle. Many Wiccans mark the north, south, east, and west with candles on the altar, space permitting. The setup of your altar will change depending on the size of your chosen space. Feel free to change any setup to fit your needs.

The Book of Shadows should also be placed on the altar, space permitting. But it may be placed on a bookstand next to the altar, or on the floor if necessary. As you can see, it is up to you to determine what is comfortable, practical, and essential for your altar.

Altar cloths can be made from the fabric of your choice and be decorated with magickal symbols. The color of the cloth may be changed for the holidays or for different rituals. Altar cloths are optional.

Choosing Space

The Earth is sacred space. The Air, the Water. There is sacred space all around us. But we all need a place of privacy to study and perform magickal work in or around our homes. Your private, sacred space will be a place of focus and learning, celebration and magick—a place where your spirit can soar and be open to the influences of the Goddess and the God and all creation.

This space may accommodate a portable altar or a permanent working altar. It can be used as a place of study, depending on its size and needs. If you live with others who are not Wiccan, let them know you will need privacy. Set up a permanent space if you are fortunate enough to have an unused room or corner of a room. If not, a temporary space will do.

Decorate your sacred space any way you wish. You may want to match the decorations to the change of seasons. Find a cabinet or closet for your supplies and decorations. You may need extra shelving for tools, props, and statuary, and a desk for your notebooks, journals, and other writing supplies. Find bookcases and have fun filling them. Get a big overstuffed reading chair, and make sure to set up adequate lighting. This is your place for learning and work; make it yours, make it comfortable and easy to work in.

If your space is limited, a corner of a bedroom or living room may be used. If you feel the need to partition off the space when it is not in use, a room divider works nicely. Set up a small table with a cloth, and basic altar supplies if you wish. You will probably find yourself spreading out into the room if your housemates know you are Wiccan.

If you are not able to use even a corner of a room, there are still options open to you. Nightstands, the top of a dresser, a shelf, all may be used if space is tight. If space is really at a premium, even a windowsill will do. You will not have the space for all the items you may wish to use, but there will be space for a symbol of the Goddess and the God and the directions and elements.

Outdoor Space

For outdoor space, be sure to have fencing, trees, or shrubs to obscure the neighbors' view of your yard. Stone benches may be used for seating and altar space. A sacred-space garden with statuary would be quite wonderful. Design your own "Witches Garden." Buy field guides and study the plants found in your area. As you learn about them, add them to your garden. This is a great way to get children to appreciate the wonders of the earth.

Choose your space wisely and with care, and you will be rewarded with something very special. It will be a place for uninterrupted learning, celebration, and joy.

MAGICKAL ASSOCIATIONS
OF COLOR

Color and light, like all things, are said to vibrate at different speeds. The different vibrations of various colors can be used by our brains in the rituals we perform for healing, meditations, and magick. This is called practical magick. Each color represents a traditional principle or value and may be used to increase our awareness.

Remember, these are traditional color associations. If you feel that you should be working with a different color than the one that is given, feel free to go with your choice. Wiccans are free to make associations that are appropriate to their tastes and their experiences.

Silver is traditionally associated with telepathy, clairvoyance, psychometry, intuition, dreams, tapping into astral energies, and the power of women and the Goddess. Other associations concern helping where there is an impasse, and being neutral in a particular situation.

Gold and yellow are associated with the God, masculine power and strength, winning, and playful humor. Work with gold or yellow when in need of charm, confidence, and persuasion.

Yellow is also connected to the sun, intelligence, learning and memory, and logic. Use yellow for magick regarding health and vigor, too.

Copper works wonders for magick that relates to professional growth and financial goals, business, and career strategies.

Orange has associations similar to copper. In addition to business and career goals, orange relates to property deals, ambition, and general success. Legal matters are also linked with this color. Use orange for encouragement, adaptability, and attraction.

Red is the color of energy, strength, passion, love, lust, and survival.

The associations of purple include the third eye, psychic ability, spiritual power, self-assurance, and hidden knowledge. Use purple for its connections to tension, power, and ambition. This color is associated with both the Goddess and the God.

Pink is identified with romantic and mature love, affection, emotional healing, good will, and nurturing. Honor and morality are also associations of this color.

Green vibrations traditionally correspond to Mother Earth, physical healing, abundance, fertility, tree and plant magick, the Element of Earth, and personal goals, finance, and luck.

Blue invites good fortune your way, and is used for magick about wisdom, spiritual inspiration, calmness and reassurance, understanding, and patience. Use it when you want to bring creativity into your life. Blue is the color of the Element of Water.

Black is the color of binding, shape-shifting, and protection. If you are confused or experiencing discord in a situation, work with the color black.

Brown has associations of friendships and special favors. Use brown if you need help being neutral in a situation. If you are uncertain or hesitant, try a ritual with a brown candle.

The associations of the color white include the Goddess, peace, spirituality, virginity in the feminine sense, and the Maiden. Use white for work concerning truth and sincerity. A white candle can be substituted for any other color if none are available.

SPELL AND RITUAL WORK

The noun *spell* as an incantation is said to be derived from a root word meaning to "speak aloud." It was not used in that context until late medieval times. The Old English word *spell* meant a narration or story. This word is also said to be the second half of the word *gospel*, which means "good tidings." When used as a verb, it is said to be from the Middle English word *spellen*, meaning "to read letter by letter."

Another meaning is related to the old English word *speld*. A speld is a thin rod of wood used to point, such as a teacher would hold. These rods were also called wands.

A spell involves words and actions chosen to achieve a certain goal or desire, and is driven by the will of the person performing it. Words, symbols, and tools are combined to produce a ritual. Power is raised and directed out to the Universe to do its work. The wand or hand focuses the energy that has been bound together. This is the origin of the term *spellbinding*.

65

On the Writing of Spells and Rituals

There are a few important things to remember when working with spells. First: There are no guarantees. Keep in mind the Rule of Three (see page 16), write with care, and do not perform a spell for someone without his or her permission.

Spells are more effective when you write your own. There are books that can introduce you to the art of spell writing, complete with charts and descriptions of magickal associations. When the spell is written by you, your energy, emotions, and essence go into it. It may seem a daunting task at the beginning, but the power and the magick is all within you now. You just have to learn to express it to the Universe.

If you find a prewritten spell or ritual that appeals to you, always feel free to adapt it to fit your goal. Modify words and props so that the spell better reflects your intention. What works for some may not work for you. We creatures of the earth are all individuals and we express ourselves differently.

Ask yourself, "What is the goal of my spell or ritual? What do I want to accomplish?" Write your intention on a slip of paper. Choose how to word your goal carefully. Precision is important in the outcome of the spell. And remember: Do not influence another or influence in a negative manner.

Decide how and when the working is to be performed. Do you require a waxing moon, or a waning one? Choose the symbols and articles that associate with the goal you have in mind. Select candles of the appropriate colors; pick out runes, beads, gems, herbs, salt, incense, or music that will help you effect a focused intention. Choose appropriate deities if you wish to work with them. You may have to do some research to find the correct ones to evoke. Or, you may wish to work with the energy of the Universe. You must decide whether to use candle magick, or moon, herbal, sympathetic, or other forms of magick. Perhaps you will use a combination of these magicks. All of these elements, either separate or together, take everyday ideas and convert them to the necessary magickal symbols to get you in the right frame of mind for spell working. You will be "setting the stage" for your spell.

When you have your components, now is the time to put it all together. This is where you decide how the spell or ritual will be performed. In what order will you light candles, and what will you be doing with those candles? Will you memorize the words you have written or chosen, or will you read them aloud? If you have trouble with this step, find a spell with a structure you like and adapt that one to your needs.

Language is crucial in the performance of spells and rituals. One mispronounced word, the wrong tone or inflection may change the intent of your spell. If you wish to do your work in a foreign language, be prepared to master the language you choose: You will need to speak it fluently. Generally, it is best to leave foreign-language magick to ceremonial magicians. In Wicca, there is no need to be so theatrical.

Performance

Take the time to cleanse, bless, and charge props and tools. This may be done in a separate ritual or just before the working is to be performed. Make sure you start fresh to release random and leftover energy from previous spells. Be physically prepared. Ground, center, and meditate. Take a ritual bath if you wish. Let your imagination soar.

All this will take time, practice, and lots of research. Your most important tool is a belief in yourself. Do not be afraid of what is inside you, but learn to release it. You may make mistakes at first—we all do—but be persistent, and you will be successful!

Tools for Writing Spells

Find a nice fountain pen or quill pen to write your spells. Invest in some colored inks. Draw a picture of your wishes and desires, or use photographs. Use your imagination. The image you eventually come up with may be ceremonially burned or buried as an offering, or kept in a sacred place.

You may want to go to antique shops or estate sales to look for these tools. You should be able to find beautiful pens and inkwells that would be a wonderful addition to your supply cabinet. Colored inks can be found in any art supply shop.

The color of ink you use may influence the spell to be performed. As in color magick, ink colors have their own traditional associations, although you should always use colors that feel right to you.

> Use blue ink in spells for healing, increased mental powers, communication, wisdom, and protection.
> Use red ink in spells about sex, courage, and energy.
> Use black ink for banishing and binding rituals and spells.
> Use green ink for prosperity, abundance, and fertility spells.

You may run across an ink called Dragons' Blood, an all-purpose ink that increases the power of a spell. There is occasionally confusion on the origin of the ink. The color comes from the sap of a tree by the name of *Daemomorops draco*. It is native to the East Indies and Canary Islands. The berries produce a red coating that is used as a dye for varnishes, tinctures, and inks. There is a garden herbaceous perennial named *Sedum spurium,* or "Dragons Blood," that should not be confused with *Daemomorops*.

The Circle

Many Wiccans feel the need to cast a circle before any magick or ritual is performed. This is not necessary, although it gives many the feeling of safety and protection.

The symbolism of a circle starts at Stonehenge. It was built around 2000 B.C.E., and has been shown to be an astronomical clock and cosmic calculator. Stonehenge follows the movement of the moon, sun, and planetary constellations. Many stone circles such as Stonehenge are found around the world. These circles were also used as sacred sites, where celebration rituals and dedications took place.

At the time, astrology and astronomy were not distinct sciences. The zodiac we know today is derived from the study and practice of these arts. The word *zodiac* is taken from the Greek word *zoidiakos*, meaning "signal" or "circle," and is incorporated into the word *ziodion*, meaning "animal circle."

The circle became the symbol of perfection, representing the unity of self; the heart of humanity; the seed; the womb. Synonymous with the spiritual Wheel of Life, it represents the conscious and subconscious, Heaven and Earth, nothing and all.

In ancient Egypt, the mathematical number 0 was thought of as the number of the goddess Nut, mother of Osiris, Isis, Nephthys, and Set. It was considered holy, a place from which all knowledge came. It was the ultimate symbol of fertility and the feminine.

Native Americans have the medicine wheel or sacred hoop. It has four cardinal directions that represent various stages of growth and enlightenment. The soul must pass through these stages to complete the Good Red Road of physical life.

The circle is a feminine symbol. It is also a symbol of protection; homes, hearths, and fences have been made in the shape of a circle. In a circle, all participants of any magickal working are protected from harm and are equals.

Circle Casting

Wiccans usually cast a circle about 9 feet in diameter. This size is said to evoke the power of Mars. The circle is usually opened by walking counterclockwise around it. The counterclockwise movement is called *widdershins*, or "against the sun." Some Wiccans construct the circle with their wand, their athame, or their finger. The circle is closed by walking clockwise, or *deosil*, "the path of the sun." Some Wiccans open and close a circle by reversing these directions, opening *deosil* and closing *widdershins*. It depends on the tradition followed or one's solitary practices.

Make sure you will not be interrupted when casting your circle. Interruptions dissipate the flow of energy. If you are working inside, the room needs to be well ventilated because of the burning herbs or incense. If you or another participant has a breathing problem, you may want to substitute heated potpourri for the incense.

Divide the circle into quarters, each corresponding to a direction and element.

The Principles of the Elements

Each element is said to have polarities, or two ways it may act. They will have an active or positive mode, and a passive or negative mode.

The principles of the Element of Fire are heat and expansion. Fire is known to be constructive and creative in its active mode, and quite destructive in its passive mode. The direction associated with fire is south. This element and its direction are used for inspiration, creativity, change, intuition, sexual energy, and spirit. Its season is summer. Fire is also associated with the color red and the astrological signs Leo, Sagittarius, and Aries. Its altar symbols include burning candles, incense, and a fire in a cauldron.

The principles of the Element of Water are cold and shrinkage. Water is said to be life-giving, protective, and nourishing in its active mode, and a divider in its passive mode. The direction associated with water is west. Water represents emotions, including love and sorrow, and is represented by wells, springs, and rivers. Its season is fall. Water is also associated with the color blue and the astrological signs Scorpio, Cancer, and Pisces. Water may be represented on the altar by a bowl or cup of water, and by shells, driftwood, and seaweed.

The Element of Air balances the active and passive actions of fire and water. Air may be dry like fire, or moist like water. The direction associated with air is east. This element and its direction are used for intellect, clarity of thought, messages, wind, and breath. Its season is spring. Air is also associated with the color yellow and the astrological signs Aquarius, Libra, and Gemini. Air may be represented on the altar by feathers, an empty bowl, and incense.

The Element of Earth is related to fire, water, and air. It consists of all of the others in a solid form. Earth is heavy and solid. The direction associated with earth is north. Earth represents fertility, abundance, work, the body, and nature. Its season is winter. Earth is also associated with the colors green or black and the astrological signs Taurus, Virgo, and Capricorn. Earth may be represented on the altar with herbs, stones, flowers, and the pentacle.

The *Akasha*, also known as the life force, is the basic substance of the universe, and all the other elements are derived from it. It pervades all, yet it is also the basis of everything that exists.

In some traditions and magickal systems, the elements are said to be populated by a type of spiritual creature known as an elemental. Gnomes, sylphs, salamanders, and undines are elementals. The gnomes populate the Element of Earth and are seen as "little people," or green light. They are the givers of stability and material gain. They also protect circles cast outdoors. Sylphs are of the Element of Air and are seen as fairies or white light. They hold the keys to knowledge, dreams, and wishes, and are protectors of magickal applications. The salamanders inhabit the Element of Fire and may be seen as dragons or lizards. They are protectors of the home or business. Undines, of the Element of Water, may be "merpeople," sirens, or pink light. Undines are protectors of the gates of death and karma.

Casting the Circle and Calling the Quarters

Supplies for the circle casting:

> 2 white altar candles
> Bowl of salt
> 4 white candles for the east, south, west,
>   and north
> Chalice or cup of water
> Bell
> Incense

Set the white candles at the east, south, west, and north points along your proposed circle. Light the altar candles. Light the incense. Ring the bell three times. Move clockwise around the circle starting at the east.

At the east candle say:

> "In lighting this Candle of the East, I bring freedom of Spirit, Powers of the East, Light and Air to this Circle I cast."

Light the candle.

At the south candle say:

> "In lighting this Candle of the South, I bring Illumination and Inspiration, Powers of the South, to this Circle I cast."

Light the candle.

At the west candle say:

> "In lighting this Candle of the West, I bring the cleansing of Water, and courage, Powers of the West, to this Circle I cast."

Light the candle.

At the north candle say:

> "In lighting this Candle of the North, I bring
> Growth and the Powers of the North, to this
> Circle I cast."

Light the candle. Visualize energy building in the circle as a blue-white light. Feel and see the energy swirling around you. Feel and see it build. Feel it build over your head and then enter your body. Visualize the energy move down and enter your arm to your dominant hand. As you walk the circle again, focus the energy through and out of your forefinger.

As you walk, say:

> "I work to cast this Circle as a safe and sacred
> space for the work of my Craft."

End at the east and say:

> "So mote it be."

At the altar, take the bowl of salt, place your index finger in it, and say:

> "I purify this salt and drive out any impurities,
> that I may use it in my workings. So mote it be."

Add three pinches of salt to the water and say:

> "Let this purifying salt drive out any impurities
> in this water, that I may use it for my work-
> ings. So mote it be."

With the water move east, clockwise, sprinkling it around the edge of the circle and say:

> "With this purifying water I bless and conse-
> crate this circle. So mote it be."

Move back to the altar, light your incense, go the east, moving clockwise and say:

> "You are welcome, Element of Air. Light and
> Air, the Powers of the East, be welcome and
> join me in this circle."

At the south:

> "You are welcome, Element of Fire. Illumi-
> nation and Inspiration, the Powers of the
> South, be welcome and join me in this circle."

At the west:

> "You are welcome, Element of Water. Cleans-
> ing Water and Courage, the Powers of the
> West, be welcome and join me in this circle."

At the north:

> "You are welcome, Element of Earth. Growth
> and the Powers of the North, be welcome and
> join me in this circle."

> "Welcome to the Four Quarters and the pow-
> ers they represent. The circle is now cast. So
> mote it be!"

Closing the Circle

To close a circle, just reverse the opening process.

Go to the white candle at the north and say:

> "Thank you and Farewell to the Element of Earth. I thank you for the Powers of the North."

Snuff out the candle.

Go to the white candle at the west and say:

> "Thank you and Farewell to the Element of Water. I thank you for the Powers of the West."

Snuff out the candle.

Go to the white candle at the south and say:

> "Thank you and Farewell to the Element of Fire. I thank you for the Powers of the South."

Snuff out the candle.

Go to the white candle at the east and say:

> "Thank you and Farewell to the Element of Air. I thank you for the Powers of the East.

> "Thank you and Farewell to the Four Quarters and the Powers they contain."

Snuff out the candle.

> "The circle is now closed. So mote it be."

Ring the bell three times.

4

Herbal Magick, Herbal Healing

WHAT IS AN HERB?

What do you think of when someone says the word *herb*? Do you think of basil, chives, and thyme? Or do you think of a quaking aspen tree and columbine flowers and clover?

Herbs have been defined as any plant that is valued for its medicinal, savory, or aromatic qualities. That covers a lot of plants. Almost every plant has been used at some point in human history. People experimented with all plants—not just with the common culinary plants but also with trees, flowers, roots, seeds, vegetables, fruits, nuts, shrubs, and berries. So, for our purposes, an herb is any plant with culinary, aromatic, remedial, veterinary, cosmetic, or domestic use.

The word *herb* is from the old Sanskrit *bharb*, meaning "to eat." This in turn became the Latin word *berba*, meaning "grass" or "fodder."

Some people use the words *herbs* and *spices* synonymously. Spices generally refers to culinary plants in powdered form or in small bits. Most spices are from woody plants and are seeds, roots, fruits, flowers, and bark. They are usually dark in color (i.e., brown, black, or red), and are from the tropics. Their flavors are usually quite strong. Examples of spices are pepper, cinnamon, and cloves. Herbs have a more subtle flavor and come from temperate zones.

Everything on this planet carries its own energy. This energy vibrates at different rates in different forms. We can learn to tap into this energy, be it in crystals or plant material. The rate of vibration is determined by the chemical makeup of the plant, and its habitat, color, and scent. When choosing plants for magickal purposes, you will need to research which plants will help you in a particular situation, whether in spell work or in ritual.

In early English usage, the word *herb* was synonymous with vegetable. It later became limited to parts of the vegetable that grow above ground. For example, a potato was considered a vegetable and the leafy top was designated an herb.

Many herbs used for culinary purposes also have magickal effects (books are available with charts of herbs and their magickal applications). Historically, methods of gathering the different herbs depended on the surrounding culture. For instance, in Babylon, magickal herbs were gathered by moonlight. They were thought to contain the most power of the Moon God, named Sin, at this time.

In Wicca, some herbs are also gathered by the full moon when used for magickal purposes. For healing purposes, all are gathered in the morning when the dew has dried.

Quaking aspen *(Populus tremuloides)* is used for intermittent fevers. It has been used as a diuretic, and as a treatment for gonorrhea. An infusion of the bark is said to be helpful for chronic diarrhea, and is a safe substitute for Peruvian bark. The traditional uses for quaking aspen include stomach or liver disorders, arthritis, benign prostatic hypertrophy, common cold, cystitis, diarrhea, dysentery, dyspepsia, fibrositis, flatulence, inflammation, and rheumatoid arthritis. Native American uses of this plant include root bark tea for excessive menstrual flow; poultices made of the root for cuts and wounds; and a tea made of the inner bark for venereal disease, stomach pain, urinary ailments, worms, colds, and fevers.

Whether you use herbs for medicinal, culinary, or magickal purposes, they are a wonderful addition to any garden. They may be grown for their foliage, and also for their flowers. Many herbs have flowers that beautify the garden landscape. So many wild plants that people consider weeds are actually herbs and can be integrated into the landscape and into your magickal garden. Recently, I went to a local nursery. I bought a White Swan echinacea that just happened to have "weeds" growing in the same pot. The bonus plant was mugwort (*Artemisia vulgaris*), which has medicinal uses for menstrual pain and menopausal problems. It also may be used magickly for strength, protection, healing, and astral projection. It was a great deal for the price of one plant!

HOW DO HERBS HEAL?

Constituents

What makes a juniper plant help an upset stomach and wood betony relieve menstrual pain? It seems the Great Mother has provided well for her children. It is said that for every human sickness, there is a plant that will cure it. This is because each plant contains chemical compounds that are known as constituents. These compounds are what give herbs their healing qualities. The following is a list of some plant constituents you will come across in herbal preparations and an example of an herb that contains it.

Alkaloids are found in roots, leaves, and seeds of some herbs. Some alkaloids are helpful in fighting bacteria, and some assist in healing fungal infections. One well-known alkaloid is atropine, a constituent known to have antispasmodic properties. It is found in the nightshade family, the family of the infamous poison belladonna (*Atropa belladonna*). Therapeutic doses of herb preparations with this alkaloid are potentially poisonous. It is best to avoid this family when working with herbs for home use. Motherwort (*Leonurus cardiaca*) also contains alkaloids. Motherwort is used in infusions, syrups, douches, eyewashes, tinctures, and decoctions. It is used for menstrual pain, the pain and excess bleeding of childbirth, and conjunctivitis.

The constituents found in herbs are called "active ingredients" by pharmacists. An herbalist uses the whole plant and does not concentrate on individual chemicals. Because plants contain so many different chemicals, each may work on more than one physical complaint. The actions of an herb may be subtle and use all of the constituents, or may be very direct and use the constituent that is most abundant. An herb may be used as is, or combined with other plants. Science has not yet explained exactly how herbs work in the body.

81

Anthraquinones, found in roots and leaves, are used to stimulate bile production and aid in digestive problems. The plant rhubarb (*Rheum palmatum*), for example, contains this constituent and is used for constipation because the anthraquinone is a gastrointestinal irritant and stimulates movement. Rhubarb is also used as a tincture, decoction, and wash. The wash is used for boils on the skin.

Bitters stimulate the flow of bile and digestive juices. They, too, can be found in roots and leaves. The common plant wormwood (*Artemisia absinthium*) contains this constituent. In the past, wormwood was used to make the drink known as absinthe. Today, bitters effectively address gallbladder and liver complaints, loss of appetite, bruises, skin problems, and menstrual pain. The aerial parts of the plant are used in infusions, decoctions, tinctures, and washes.

82

According to Ayurvedic medicine, India's ancient healing tradition, the body contains energy, known as *prana*. This energy brings life to the body and the mind. Ayurveda uses diet and exercise to bring more of this energy to the body. The five elements of Earth, Air, Fire, Water, and Ether are converted by *agni*. *Agni* is the digestive fire, and helps to form three personality types, called *doshas*. The *vata* personality is active, restless, and alert. The *pitta* is creative and competitive, and the *kapha* is slow-moving and strong. Foods, herbs, and exercise are used to bring the doshas back in balance at times of illness.

Cyanogenic glycosides are said to be soothing to the lungs and heart, and are used for coughs and nausea. Saint-John's-wort (*Hypericum perforatum*) contains glycosides. It has been used for anxiety, nervous tension, emotional upsets, depression, sciatica, and skin problems. Saint-John's-wort is used in infusions, tinctures, creams, and infused oils, and as a wash.

Flavonoids are found in flowers, leaves, stems, fruit, and roots of some herbs. This constituent protects cells from oxidation damage, eases water retention, and helps with inflammation and muscle spasms. Self-heal (*Prunella vulgaris*), a blue-flowered Eurasian mint, contains flavonoids. Self-heal is used for inflammation of the mouth and sore throat. The aerial parts of the plant are used in tinctures, infusions, poultices, ointments, and gargles.

83

Gums and resins have been found useful in treating high cholesterol. These constituents are found in the sap of trunks and branches of some trees and shrubs. The shrub known as myrrh (*Commiphora molmol*) contains resins and gums. Myrrh is used for glandular fevers, sore throat, ulcers of the mouth, and upper respiratory problems, and is used externally on wounds. Myrrh may be used in tinctures, in capsules, as a gargle, and as an essential oil and powder.

Lectins are glycoproteins found most readily in the leaves of the family of *Fabaceae*, the common bean. Lectins stimulate the immune system and have anticancer properties. Pokeweed (*Phytolacca americana*) contains this constituent and has been used to treat skin sores and abscesses, for relief of the inflammation of arthritis, and as a laxative. It is used as a tincture, decoction, syrup, ointment, and poultice.

As with most herbalists, the Arabs believed that nature provided cures to all ills. They researched plants in their country and surrounding lands. The Arab physicians were also businessmen, opening the first pharmacies and shops as early as the ninth century. They were also the first to use astrology for diagnosis of illness and treatment.

84

Mucilage soothes irritated mucous membranes, and so is used to ease constipation. You will find mucilage in seeds, roots, and the inner bark of certain herbs. A great source of this constituent is marshmallow (*Althaea officinalis*). This plant is used as an expectorant, and for urinary disorders, cystitis, inflammations of the mucous membranes of the urinary and digestive systems, skin wounds, and inflammations. Marshmallow is used in syrups, infusions, decoctions, tinctures, ointments, and poultices.

Oxalates are salts of oxalic acid and are found in the *Oxalidaceae* family. Oxalates are known for their sour taste. These salts shorten the time it takes for blood to coagulate. They are used during surgery to control bleeding. The plant wood sorrel (*Oxalis acetosella*) contains oxalates and was once used for digestive disorders. Wood sorrel is no longer used as an herbal medication.

Saponins are found in roots, stems, and leaves. Some help to reduce coughs or act as expectorants; others regulate hormones and strengthen blood vessels. Some are also gastrointestinal irritants that are used to stimulate the function of the gastrointestinal tract and are used sparingly. Sweet violet (*Viola odorata*) may be used for coughs, infections of the mouth and throat, digestive disorders, and skin rashes, and as a stimulant for the circulatory and immune systems. Violet is used in syrups, mouthwashes, infusions, tinctures, poultices, and creams.

In Europe, during the Renaissance, local women herbalists known as wise women acted as family physicians. They were making preparations, compiling notes, and passing information and recipes from mother to daughter, from generation to generation. Every town had its own wise woman that the locals would visit in times of need.

85

Salicylates are salts of salicylic acid and are found in bark, leaves, and flowers. These salts are mild analgesics and anti-inflammatories. One familiar herb with salicylates is meadowsweet (*Filipendula ulmaria*). Meadowsweet has been used for feverish colds, upset stomachs, gastric ulcers, arthritis pain, and conjunctivitis. It is used as an infusion, an eyewash, and a tincture, and in a compress.

Tannins have an astringent action that protects and heals mucous membranes and skin. Tannins may be found in bark, roots, fruits, and seeds and leaves of plants, especially of the oak family *Fagaceae*. The percentage of tannins is greatest in the galls found on these trees. Tannins may also be found in agrimony (*Agrimonia eupatoria*), a gentle remedy for diarrhea, cystitis, urinary infections, bronchitis, migraines, eczema, conjunctivitis, and sore throats. Tannins are used in infusions, tinctures, poultices, washes, and gargles.

Volatile oils relieve stress in aromatherapy, enhance appetite, stimulate circulation, have an antiseptic action, and relieve water retention. The oil is found in bark, stems, and leaves. The cowslip species (*Primula* spp.) is known for the volatile oils found in its flowers. Cowslip has been used for headaches, chills, insomnia, anxiety, sunburn, skin blemishes, and chronic bronchitis. It is used in infusions, compresses, and ointments, and in essential oil form.

During the Middle Ages, midwives in Europe used contaminated rye that carried ergot, a common fungus found on grain and cereals. This fungus is a uterine stimulant and caused swift births with less blood loss. Ergot is still sometimes used by midwives.

Medicinal Actions

In your studies of herbal medicines, you will come across the term *actions*. Every herb you take into your body will have an effect on it; this is what is meant by action. Actions are caused by the chemical constituents found in herbs. Never ingest an herb without knowing what effects it may have on your body. The following is a list of some of the terms you may encounter in your studies.

Alteratives restore health and vitality to an ailing body. Some plants with the action of an alterative improve the ability to eliminate body waste, others stimulate digestive actions. One plant used as an alterative is stinging nettles (*Urtica dioca*). The leaves and stalks of stinging nettles may be used as an infusion, decoction, or tincture. The plant's characteristic stinging will be lost when cooked.

> The ancient Greeks had two different styles of healing the body. One style was known as temple healing. An ill person would go to a temple for help. These temples were usually set in the countryside and contained gardens of healing plants and sacred trees. Treatment was given in the form of herbs, massage, exercise, and a proper diet in combination with prayers and rituals. The other style of healing was known as rational healing. This style—Hippocrates' way of healing—is considered the beginning of modern herbal medicine.

Anti-inflammatories help fight inflammation. There are said to be three types of plants with this action. One contains an aspirin-like chemical known as salicylate. Some contain steroids. There are also plants that are not understood; the basis for their action is unknown. Bark of the willow (*Salix alba*) contains the salicin substance and is used as an anti-inflammatory. Use willow in a decoction or tincture.

Antispasmodics may ease or prevent muscle spasms and cramps. Plants with this action reduce muscle tension. Use the bark of cramp bark (*Viburnum opulus*) by itself or combined with prickly ash or wild yam in a decoction or tincture to ease cramps.

Carminatives stimulate the digestive system and are rich in oils. Gingerroot (*Zingiber officinale*) has been used as a carminative. Use ginger in an infusion, decoction, or tincture.

A demulcent is rich in mucilage. These plants soothe irritated or inflamed tissue, either inside the body or out. An example of a demulcent is comfrey (*Symphytum officinale*). It has been used for gastric ulcers, and to soothe lungs irritated by coughs. Comfrey is also used for healing external wounds. It may be combined with marshmallow and meadowsweet, and used in infusions, decoctions, and tinctures. For bronchial trouble, it may be combined with coltsfoot or horehound.

Chinese herbal medicine is based on the idea that the body is made up of the five Elements of Wood, Fire, Earth, Metal, and Water. Each of these elements has associations to seasons, emotions, and parts of the body. The elements need to be in balance in the body for continued good health, as they are interconnected. Wood promotes fire, fire gives way to earth, earth furnishes metal, metal produces water, and water brings wood. Healing herbs are prescribed to bring back balance in the case of illness.

Diaphoretics promote sweating, which eliminates waste from the body. Boneset (*Eupatorium perfoliatum*) has this action. Use the leaves and stems as a simple (i.e., an herbal remedy using only the single herb) or combined with yarrow, elder flowers, or cayenne in tinctures or infusions.

Diuretics increase the amount of urine excreted by the body by increasing blood flow to the kidneys. This added blood flow increases the amount of urine produced. Some diuretics work by their constituents being excreted by the kidneys. This produces a change in osmosis causing more water to be lost by the body. An example of a diuretic is couch grass, also known as quack grass and witchgrass (*Agrophyron repens*). Use it in a decoction or tincture.

89

Emetics have been used with purgatives and diaphoretics. The action of an emetic is to cleanse the body's systems and to remove poisonous materials before the body has a chance to absorb them. Blue flag (*Iris versicolor*), a common blue-flowered iris, has emetic action. Its rootstock is used in an infusion or tincture.

Emmenagogues are uterine stimulants, used to promote menstrual discharge. They also may strengthen muscle tone and glandular tissue, and are known to increase blood supply to the uterus. Modern western medicine does not always recognize the actions of emmenagogues. Plants with this action may produce miscarriage and are never to be used during pregnancy. Rosemary (*Rosmarinus officinalis*) is an emmenagogue; its leaves may be used in an infusion.

An emollient will soothe, soften, and protect skin. These plants usually contain mucilage or oil, great skin softeners. Use greater plantain (*Plantago major*) as an emollient. The leaves and stalks are used in ointments and poultices.

Expectorants help remove excess mucus from the lungs. Some work by irritating the lining of the bronchioles. This stimulates removal of the mucus by using the reflex action caused by the constituent of the plant, most often saponin. An example would be ipecac. Other expectorants have a relaxing effect and soothe bronchial spasms. Using the constituents of mucilage or oils, they thin and loosen the mucus. Mullein (*Verbascum thapsus*) is considered an expectorant and may be used as a simple or with white horehound. Use the leaves and flowers as an infusion or tincture.

Hepatics work in various ways to affect the liver. They strengthen and increase bile flow (an action that is not entirely understood). An example of an hepatic is dandelion (*Taraxacum officinale*). Use the roots and leaves as a simple or combined with barberry in decoctions and tinctures.

A hypnotic will induce a deep, healing sleep by relaxing the muscles of the body or using alkaloids they may contain to act directly on the central nervous system. The plant known as hops (*Humulus lupulus*) is a remedy for insomnia. Use the flowers as a simple, or with valerian or passionflower in an infusion or tincture to help you sleep.

Gastrointestinal irritants irritate and inflame the GI tract. Plants that effect this action have been used to encourage function of the tract; the irritation is usually an unwanted side effect. Bloodroot (*Sanguinaria canadensis*) has uses as an expectorant and emetic, but has the side effect of a GI irritant and should never be used without supervision.

A laxative stimulates the large intestine and speeds up bowel movements. Plants with this effect on the body contain the constituent anthraquinone glycoside and promote greater contractions of the large intestine. A laxative is not meant for prolonged or long-term use. The bark of the butternut tree (*Juglans cinerea*) may be used in a decoction as a laxative.

Apply a rubefacient to the skin to cause a gentle increase in blood to an area. This is done to ease the pain and swelling of arthritis. Ground seed of the mustard plant (*Brassica alba*) may be used in a poultice. Bruised seed may be used in a footbath.

Sedatives are used to calm the nervous system, and many also are hypnotics. The terms are considered almost synonymous. Some plants with this action may have specific constituents, but more research is needed to totally understand this group. Wild lettuce (*Lactuca virosa*) may be used as a sedative, as a simple, or combined with valerian. Combine it with skullcap for stress. Use the leaves of wild lettuce in an infusion or tincture.

Stimulants cause an increase of activity to parts of the spinal cord and brain. The long-term use of a stimulant may cause nervousness, headaches, tremors, and insomnia. The most common form of a stimulant is the alkaloid caffeine, found in coffee, most teas, and some sodas.

Tonics are used to strengthen the whole body or target certain organs. The reason for a tonic's action is not entirely understood. Goldenseal (*Hydrastis canadensis*) makes a good tonic. Mix it with meadowsweet or chamomile for stomach conditions. Use goldenseal flowers in infusions, tinctures, and poultices.

Vulneraries are used to help in the healing of internal or external wounds or inflammation. Plants with this action contain tannins or mucilage. Use pot marigold (*Calendula officinalis*) to treat skin problems, wounds, burns, and ulcers. Flowers of marigold are used in infusions, tinctures, and poultices.

OTHER TYPES OF MEDICINAL ACTIONS

ACTION	DESCRIPTION
Anodyne	Relieves pain
Anthelmintic	Expels worms
Anthilic	Prevents formation of urinary stones
Antiemetic	Stops vomiting
Antiepileptic	Helps in the relief of seizures
Antisyphilitic	Helps or cures sexually transmitted diseases
Aperient	Provides gentle laxative action
Astringent	Causes contraction or tightening effect
Cathartic	Promotes bowel evacuation
Cephalic	Works for diseases of the head
Cholagogue	Increases flow of bile
Deobstruent	Removes obstruction
Detergent	Cleanses (used for boils, ulcers, wounds, and the like)
Discutient	Heals tumors
Febrifuge	Reduces fever
Herpatic	Helps any skin disease
Lithontryptic	Dissolves urinary organ calculi
Maturating	Brings boils to a head
Nervine	Targets the nervous system

ACTION	DESCRIPTION
Ophthalmicum	Helps in the relief of eye diseases
Parturient	Induces and promotes labor
Pectoral	Works for chest infections
Refrigerant	Has a cooling effect
Resolvent	Dissolves boils
Sedative	Settles nerves and promotes sleep
Sialogogue	Increases saliva secretion
Stomachic	Relieves indigestion
Styptic	Stops bleeding
Tonic	Provides an overall remedy that is invigorating and strengthening
Vermifuge	Expels worms from the body

Healing Herbs

The following is only a short list of the herbs that are available to use as healing plants. If used for healing by itself, the herbal remedy is called a simple. The following herbs may be used as simples or with a combination of other herbs. Remember, do not ingest any herb without knowing what its action is. Some are known to cause allergic reactions.

Ailment	Herb	Combinations	Part of Herb Used	Preparations*
Acne	Blue flag (*Iris versicolor*)	Echinacea, burdock, yellow dock	Rhizome	Decoction, tincture
Allergic rhinitis	Eyebright (*Euphrasia officinalis*)	Goldenseal, elderflower	Aerial parts	Infusion, tincture
Anemia	Stinging nettle (*Urtica dioica*)	Use as a simple	Aerial parts	Infusion
Arthritis	Willow bark (*Salix nigra*)	Angelica, black cohosh, yellow dock	Bark	Decoction, tincture
	White poplar (*Populus tremuloides*)	Use as a simple	Bark	Decoction, tincture
Bronchitis	Elecampane (*Inula helenium*)	Horsetail, hyssop, white horehound	Root	Decoction, syrup, tincture
Coughs	Hyssop (*Hyssopus officinalis*)	Elecampane, white horehound	Aerial parts	Infusion, tincture

Condition	Herb	Combinations	Part used	Preparation
Diarrhea	American cranesbill *(Geranium maculatum)*	Marshmallow root, meadowsweet, burnet	Rhizome	Infusion, decoction
Dysmenorrhea, menstrual cramps	Cramp bark *(Viburnum opulus)*	Prickly ash, wild yam	Bark	Decoction, tincture
Earache	Mullein *(Verbascum thapsus)*	Use as a simple	Flowers	Cool infusion used as ear drops
Eczema	Burdock *(Arctium lappa)*	Nettles, red clover	Leaves	Decoction, tincture
Fever	Yarrow *(Achillea millefolium)*	Use as a simple	Aerial parts	Infusion, tincture
Heartburn	Meadowsweet *(Filipendula ulmaria)*	Use as a simple	Aerial parts	Infusion, tincture
Hemorrhoids	Pilewort *(Ranunculus ficaria)*	Use as a simple	Leaves, root	Infusion, tincture
Hives	Cabbage *(Brassica oleracea)*	Use as a simple	Leaves	Apply crushed leaf to area of skin affected, or use in lotion form

continued on next page

Ailment	Herb	Combinations	Part of Herb Used	Preparations*
Incontinence, bed-wetting	Horsetail (*Equisetum arvense*)	Use as a simple	Aerial parts	Infusion, tincture
Irritable bowel syndrome	Chamomile (*Chamaemelum nobile*)	Peppermint, ginger	Flowers	Infusion, tincture
Muscle sprains and strains	Arnica (*Arnica montana*)	Use as a simple	Flowers	Tincture, compress (do not use on broken skin)
Nausea	Cloves (*Syzygium aromaticum*)	Use as a simple	Flowers, flower buds	Infusion of flower buds
Premenstrual syndrome (PMS)	Lady's mantle (*Alchemilla vulgaris*)	Black cohosh, mugwort, dead nettle	Aerial parts	Tincture, infusion
Prostate problems	Saw palmetto (*Serenoa repens*)	Use as a simple	Berries	Decoction, tincture
Sinusitis	Ground ivy (*Glechoma hederacea*)	Use as a simple	Leaves	Infusion, tincture

Tension headache	Wood betony (*Stachys officinalis*)	Lavender, skullcap, vervain	Aerial parts	Infusion, tincture
Urinary tract infections	Bearberry (*Arctostaphylos uva-ursi*)	Couch grass, yarrow	Leaves	Infusion, tincture
	Couch grass (*Elymus repens*)	Bearberry, juniper	Rhizome	Infusion, tincture
Warts	Dandelion (*Taraxacum officinale*)	Use as a simple	Sap	Use the sap directly from cut stem on affected area
Water retention	Parsley (*Petroselinum sativum*)	Use as a simple	Root, leaves, seeds	Infusion, tincture
Yeast Infections	Pot marigold (*Calendula officinalis*)	Coneflower	Flowers	Infusion, tincture

*For instructions on making herbal preparations, see pages 132–144.

PLANT MAGICK

In your magickal endeavors using herbs, you will need to know their magickal associations. Some herbs may not be listed in herbal magick books, so you will need to make your own associations for these plants. There are ways to help you decide what associations you assign to your herbs. This important aspect of the Craft is known as "wort cunning." It is the knowledge of the healing and magickal properties of herbs.

In order to win over more converts to Christianity from the pagan countryside, the Church incorporated pagan celebrations and customs. For instance, many plants had magickal and spiritual associations for the pagan community. According to the Greeks, the rose was the flower of Aphrodite. The Church later reconsecrated the rose to the Virgin Mary.

Plants were also used by the Church for teaching. The herb Lady's mantle reproduces even though the male parts of the plants wilt before the female parts finish developing. The Church taught rural folk that this was a reminder of the virgin birth and of the purity of Mary. Science now understands the reproduction process of this type of plant; it is known as parthenogenesis.

There are books on the market that contain folklore and bits of trivia on local plant life. Search out some of them. You should be able to find a piece of folklore that will help in the assigning of associations. You may run across a tale of healing, love, protection, or fertility power and continue your associations from there. For instance, if, according to the lore you have found, a local plant is a healing plant, assign it healing powers. If it has a soft effect of the feminine, give it the feminine association. The feminine planet association for a healing herb would then be the Moon. The element that is associated with healing is Earth. You now have magickal associations for a plant not listed in your magickal books!

99

GENDER ASSOCIATIONS

GENDER	ASSOCIATED PROPERTIES/USES
Male	Strong vibrations. Uses include protection, purification, hex-breaking, lust, maintaining sexual potency, health, strength, and courage
Female	Quieter in effects. Uses include attracting love, increasing beauty, maintaining youth, aiding in healing, developing psychic powers, increasing fertility, attracting wealth, promoting happiness and peace, fostering spirituality, causing visions

ASSOCIATIONS FOR RULING PLANETS

PLANET	ASSOCIATED PROPERTIES/USES
Sun	Legal matters, healing, protection
Moon	Sleep, prophetic dreams, fertility, peace, healing
Mercury	Mental powers, divination, psychic powers, wisdom
Venus	Love, friendship, fidelity, beauty, youth
Mars	Courage, strength, lust, sexual potency, hex-breaking, protection
Jupiter	Money, prosperity, legal matters, luck
Saturn	Visions, longevity, endings

100

ASSOCIATIONS FOR RULING ELEMENTS

ELEMENT	ASSOCIATED PROPERTIES/USES
Earth	Money, prosperity, fertility, healing, employment
Air	Mental powers, visions, psychic powers, wisdom
Fire	Lust, courage, strength, protection, health
Water	Sleep, meditation, purification, prophetic dreams, healing, love, friendships, fidelity

Another way of finding magickal associations for plants is found in the name of the plant, or the classification and nomenclature of the plant in question. All known species of plants are given a scientific, or botanical, name. For my example, I will use the plant known as bee balm (*Monarda didyma*), variety Croftway Pink.

> The Doctrine of Signatures was developed and used until the Middle Ages. According to this principle, a plant's use may be determined by its appearance and structure. Each plant was thought to give a hint, or sign, as to what illness the plant would help. A plant with a yellow flower was thought to be good for liver problems, and an herb for healing wounds had leaves in the shape of a shield, such as comfrey. Burdock was considered good for the hair because the burrs clung so easily to hair.

101

There are several layers in the name of a plant. These scientific names are always in Latin and in italics, except for variety names. This way, no matter where in the world you live, if I am writing about *Monarda didyma*, you will be able to find this exact species rather than another plant that goes by the same common name of bee balm. Bee balm, for instance, is also known as Oswego tea, bergamot, Indian Plume, fragrant balm, and mountain mint.

The scientific name makes identifying the plant easier than wading through all the common names, and then ending up with the wrong plant. The first name, *Monarda*, refers to the genus of the plant. In the nomenclature of plants, a genus is a subcategory of the family. The second name is the species name. A species is a smaller group within the genus. The species name often describes an outstanding characteristic of the plant. The species name of *didyma* is derived from a Greek word meaning "paired" or "twin." This pairing refers to the twin stamens on each of the flowers of this plant.

Native Americans had extensive knowledge of herbal medicine. The colonists were taught herbal medicines, how to set fractures, heal wounds, and help women have safer births. Plants introduced to the settlers included joe-pye weed, goldenseal, mayapple, and sassafras. Even though the natives had their own shaman that claimed the herb's use was given in a vision, they also thought that each plant gave a clue to its medicinal use in its appearance. It was their use of a Doctrine of Signatures.

The entry for *Monarda didyma* in one of my field guides does not list medicinal purposes but it does give the family name of the plant, Lamiaceae. This is the Latin name for the family of mints and is not written in italics. You may use the family group to assign your magickal associations. You will find listings for mints, such as peppermint (*Mentha piperita*), family Lamiaceae, in your magickal books. The magical associations of peppermint may be applied to any plants of the same family. The gender is masculine, the planet is Mercury, the Element is Fire, and the magickal associations include protection. If you look up spearmint, you will come up with different associations. Which will you use? I choose to use the feminine associations of spearmint for bee balm. Since the plant I was working with was the variety of bee balm known as Croftway Pink rather than the bright red wild bee balm, I chose the softer associations of the feminine spearmint.

Carl von Linné, better known as Linnaeus (1707–1778), was a Swedish scientist and botanist. Linnaeus worked on a system of classification based on the way plants reproduce. In his *System Naturae*, Linnaeus separated plants into twenty-four classes based on the number of stamens in the flowers. Each class was then arranged into orders based on the number of pistils of the flower. The functioning of the pistils and stamens then determined the genus of the plant. These were divided further into species. Linnaeus's method of classification has been streamlined and is still in use. It is known as binomial nomenclature, and uses the genus and species names.

103

In my Book of Shadows, I like to record the magickal associations I make based on my research. My entry for bee balm looks like this:

Monarda didyma

COMMON NAMES: Bee balm, bergamot, oswego tea, Indian plume, fragrant balm, mountain mint, golden Melissa, Indian nettle, blue balm, high balm, low balm, mountain balm

ELEMENT: Earth

RULING PLANET: Moon

GENDER: Feminine

MAGICKAL POWERS: Healing, love, protection, development of psychic powers

DESCRIPTION: *Monarda didyma* has a square, hairy stem. These stems are also hard and grooved and bear deep green, ovate, sharply toothed (serrated) leaves that are 3 to 6 inches long. The leaves are paired and have hairs on the lower side. This plant grows 2 to 3 feet high.

The flowers appear in large whorls at the top of the stem, supported by leafy bracts. The leaflets of the bracts are pale green tinged with red.

Other types include:

> *M. fistulosa,* common name wild bergamot.

> *M. punctata,* common name horsemint.

CULTIVATION: *Monarda* prefers full sun or light shade with rich organic soil. Propagation is easy; roots creep in all directions. This plant is also propagated by slips or cuttings. Flowers appear in July and August, through September.

Monarda is susceptible to powdery mildew, so give it space for air circulation. Zones 4–9. Soil pH 6.5.

PARTS OF THE PLANT USED: The leaves and flowers of *Monarda* are used. To harvest, cut the plant down to 1 inch above the ground as soon as the lower leaves begin to yellow. Leaves for tea are cut as needed. For the best flavor, strip the leaves from the stems and lay out to dry for 2 or 3 days in a warm shady place. If you dry them any longer than this, the leaves may discolor, producing a tea with less flavor.

PLANT ANALYSIS: *Monarda* contains thymol, an antiseptic against fungi, bacteria, and some parasites.

MEDICINAL USE: Use this plant in an infusion for coughs, sore throats, nausea, flatulence, and menstrual cramps.

MEDICINAL ACTION: Carminative, rubefacient, stimulant. Thymol from *M. punctata* is considered strongest.

DOSAGE: As an infusion: Pour a cup of boiling water onto 1 teaspoonful of the herb and infuse for about 15 minutes. Drink three times a day.

MAGICKAL USE: Use *Monarda* in spells and rituals for developing psychic powers, protection, or fertility.

HISTORY: The name *Monarda* is from Nicholas Monardes (1493–1588), a Spanish botanist. *Didyma* is from the Greek word meaning "paired or twinned." This refers to the two stamens in each flower.

Monarda was discovered by colonists in New York State. The place was named Ostego after the Native Americans that lived there. The name Ostego was often reported as Oswego. When settlers arrived, they learned of a bee balm

105

continued on next page

tea brewed by the Native Americans. It was used as a medicine and also for pleasure. This tea became popular and, during the Revolutionary War, replaced black tea. In the mid-1700s, an outpost was set on Lake Ontario by John Bartram of Philadelphia. Bartram gathered some *Monarda* seeds from the outskirts of the post and sent them to England. *Monarda* then made its way to Europe. Oil from the plant was used as soap or perfume.

LORE: None found.

CULINARY: Mix *Monarda* with Indian black tea and you have a copy of the famous Earl Grey tea. Add the fresh flowers of *Monarda* to salads or use as a garnish. It will add a citrusy taste. Use fresh, whole, or chopped leaves for duck, pork, meat sausages, and curries. The flavor of *Monarda* works well with strawberries, apples, oranges, tangerines, and melons.

While you are exploring your backyard, keep one thing in mind. Do not attempt to gather and use wild plants for medicinal purposes without having a trained or experienced person identify the plant. There are many poisonous and nonpoisonous plants that look quite similar. If you are in doubt about the identity of a plant, bring a specimen to your local cooperative extension service. Be careful, but have fun identifying and using plants found around your home. You now have more plants to work with, and you are not limited to the plants that are listed in magickal books. And they don't cost anything! Just as the ancient folk who worked with plants found them around their home, now you are able to do the same.

Bee balm spreads quite quickly by its creeping roots. Give it room to spread in a corner of the garden. If you have a small garden or want just a small patch of it you may dig the herb up every couple of years and divide it. Give away the sections. You may also contain it by setting a large potted specimen directly in the garden soil.

A Garden of Directions

Draw a circle on the ground of at least nine feet. Use a compass to find the directions of north, south, east, and west. Divide this circle into eight pie shapes so that the middle of the outside arc of four of the wedges is at one of those points. Remove the sod at the north, south, east, and west points. You may raise the beds by working the soil and adding an edging, if you wish. You may also remove the sod in the other four wedges and add paving stone or gravel.

At each point, plant herbs associated with that particular direction. Plants for the direction of north include loosestrife, mugwort, wood sorrel, horehound, and horsetail. You may also plant any herb with the association of the Element of Earth. Plants for the direction of east include agrimony, bittersweet nightshade, borage, clover, eyebright, marjoram, and sage. You may also use any herb with the association of the Element of Air, as this is the element of the east. Plants for the direction of south include pasque flower, basil, carrot, celery, cinquefoil, hyssop, mullein, and nettle. You may also use any herb with the association of the Element of Fire, as this is the element of the south. Plants for the direction of west include aster, lemon balm, bedstraw, catnip, daffodil, feverfew, Lady's mantle, and yarrow. You may also use any herb with the association of the Element of Water, as this is the element of the west.

You may wish to add a stepping stone with the directions marked on it at the center of your circle garden. These stones are normally available at your local nursery or garden centers. And if you are so inspired, you may prefer to make your own.

HEALING AND SPELL WORK

Wiccans often use herbs in spells for healing. Do research to find the appropriate herb, and once you obtain it write your spell. Never perform a healing spell for someone else without his or her permission.

There are general spells and amulets for the continuation of good health to which you can refer, as well. Plants you may use for general good health spells include coriander, garlic, lemon balm, rosemary, tansy, thyme, fennel, rue, and oak. You may carry sprigs of the herb on your body, replacing them every two months or so.

Do not substitute any herbal healing for modern health care. If you or someone you know is seriously ill, see a health-care professional.

Poppets are dolls that are sometimes used in healing spells. Cut a human figure from two pieces of cloth. Put the right sides of the fabric together and sew, leaving a small section open. Turn the fabric right-side out. Stuff the poppet with an appropriate healing herb and sew it closed. Remember, do not perform any healing spells or rituals for anyone without their consent.

Spell for General Good Health

Supplies for this spell include

> 1 of the general healing herbs in a small pot
> 1 green votive candle and holder
> You may add additional supplies of your
> choice if you are casting a circle.

As you light the green votive candle on your table or altar, recite something like:

> "Healing candle of green,
> Good health I have seen."

Pick up the plant and recite:

> "Continued good health
> is my herb's chosen wealth."

Feel the healing energy of the plant move into you. Visualize this energy as a white light flowing from the plant into you and back out again. Feel the vital energy of the plant mingle with yours and return to the plant in a constant cycle. Visualize the combined energy of you and the plant strengthening each other. Concentrate on feeling this healing energy for at least five minutes.

Set the plant down and recite something like:

> "Vital Herb and Candle in front of me,
> Good health is mine, So mote it be!"

If you have cast a circle for this spell, close it now. Let the candle burn down. Do not leave the candle unattended. If you must leave, snuff out the candle and relight it at a later time. Relighting the candle will not have an effect on the spell.

After the candle has burned down, plant the herb where it is likely to thrive in your garden and say:

> "Vital Herb of health and strength,
> Your home is here, for now and length."

> "In the earth, I set it live.
> here it will set roots and thrive."

Water the plant well and enjoy the new addition to your garden.

5

Growing, Harvesting, and Preparing Your Own Herbs

You may find that as you get more familiar with the magickal, physical, and spiritual benefits of herbs, you will want to grow your own. Herbalists often find it both fun and cost-effective: a pack of seeds will yield many young plants for a fraction of the cost of a nursery-grown plant. But, most important, the magickal potency of your plants will be increased because you put your own energy into growing and nurturing them.

When growing your own herbs, you will have to consider the following:

1. Will you be planting indoors or outdoors? If you choose to plant indoors, you will need suitable pots and certain potting supplies. If you choose to cultivate a garden, you will need basic gardening tools.

2. Do you want to grow medicinal herbs, culinary herbs, dyeing herbs, or magickal plants? Make a list of the herbs that interest you.

3. If you have chosen to plant in pots, grow only plants that do well in the confinement of containers, such as rosemary and most mints.

4. If you have chosen to start a garden, you will need to know the conditions in which plants thrive and choose accordingly. If you have a sunny garden, choose plants that like a lot of sun. Also, choose plants that have similar needs and group them together in the garden. Write down germination times if you are growing plants from seed.

Terra-cotta or plastic, ceramic or metal— which type of material makes a better pot? Terra-cotta, also known as clay, does have a few advantages. Clay pots are heavy and not easily knocked over by wind; they breathe well; they do not overheat as quickly as other kinds; and they are attractive in any kind of garden. But terra-cotta also has some disadvantages. Because it breathes so well, terra-cotta loses moisture from the soil much quicker than, say, plastic (which holds water better but is much less attractive). Plus terra-cotta (and other ceramic pots) may be easily broken.

As for metal containers, they should not be used in sunny areas as the heat may burn plant roots.

A warning about growing mints: Even though mints are wonderful plants, they will quickly take over a garden. They are quite invasive and should therefore remain contained. If you feel you must have mints in your garden, confine their root systems in a pot to keep them from becoming a nuisance.

PLANTING AND MOON PHASE

Growing plants has long been associated with the magick of the moon. Many cultures have lore about when to plant and when to harvest. Some studies have shown that planting by the phases of the moon will indeed work wonders. Generally, it is best to plant two days before the full moon, especially the seeds of double-flowered plants, but no later than three days after the full moon.

Astrology has also been used in conjunction with the moon phase for planting and harvesting purposes. Plant your garden during the new or waxing moon when it is in the fertile signs of Cancer, Scorpio, Pisces, Taurus, Capricorn, and Libra. If you are planting root crops, use the waxing or full moon while in Taurus. The best time to plant your herb garden is when the new or waxing moon is in the most fertile signs of Cancer, Pisces, Taurus, and Capricorn. For example, it is said that if you want the best sage, plant it with the full moon in Pisces, Scorpio, or Cancer. If you are planting flowers for fragrance, plant when the moon's first quarter is in the sign of Libra.

Plan to harvest during the waxing of the moon because the plants' vital energy rises at this time. It is the best time to gather leaves, stalks, and flowers.

If you wish to harvest roots, either for culinary or medicinal purposes, the waning moon is the optimal time. It is also the ideal time to eradicate insect pests from the garden and to weed. Use the waning moon in the barren signs of Leo, Gemini, Virgo, Sagittarius, and Aries.

The barren signs of the zodiac are the best times for plowing and cultivation of the land. Make your herbal preparations using the positive energy of the waxing moon or, if the goal is to banish illness, use the waning moon's energies. Stir your preparations clockwise if you wish, to include the blessing of the sun.

114

> The Swiss alchemist Paracelsus (1493–1541) claimed herbs used for medicinal purposes should be harvested when the moon was in Virgo, but not with Jupiter ascending.

If you are unsure of the moon phase, you can check on most calendars. If you wish to know when the moon is in a certain sign, look it up in an almanac (these are available at grocery stores, garden centers, and bookstores).

Experiment with planting times and record your findings in your Book of Shadows. Suggestions passed down from other herbalists or found in reference books are not laws, but guides. You may certainly plant at other times, and harvest whenever your plants are ready.

GROWING PLANTS INDOORS

If you've done your research and chosen plants that can thrive in containers and indoors, you will find them to require little maintenance, especially if you heed the following tips.

Grow a few herbs in pots on a sill in a sunny window. Be sure the plants get at least four to six hours of sun daily.

If you have a home that is angled on the property in such a way that it receives no direct sun through any windows, there is a great alternative available to you: fluorescent lights. The grow lights you find in garden shops can be quite expensive; regular shop lights (fluorescent lights) are a fine alternative for growing plants indoors. But note that the plants will need between fourteen and sixteen hours daily under the lights (the equivalent of four to six hours of natural sunlight).

Note that if you are growing tall seedlings, the fluorescent lights are inadequate when situated more than 12 inches above the plant. The plants get leggy and tend to topple. Start these seedlings two to three weeks later than you normally would. Then set them outside after the last frost.

Fluorescent bulbs are available in different shades of light. Cool white bulbs will emit a bright bluish-white light. Warm light will give a pinkish glow. Natural white is a whiter light, and day-light bulbs simulate the light of a sunny day. These different lights are produced by coating the interior of the tube with different fluorescent powders. You may use any combination of fluorescent tubes for growing plants. Rotate your flats for better growth under the lights, as the light is weaker near the ends of the tubes.

You will need adjustable shelving. The young plants will need to be 4–5 inches away from the light source. Adjust the shelves as necessary as the plants grow. Or, if you prefer, raise the light if it is movable.

GROWING HERBS FROM SEED

Most herbalists find it truly gratifying to grow their own herbs from seed and then transplant them to a loving home in a garden. Seeds are just one of the miracles of nature. They carry the promise of new life and beauty. All they require is a little tender loving care to get them off to a good start.

What magick is contained in a seed! Science describes the process the following way. When water is absorbed by the seed, the pressure ruptures the seed coat. This creates a break for the eruption of the root and stem. The seed undergoes metabolic changes; the food stored in the endosperm is ready to feed the seedling. The plant embryo in the seed resembles a short stem with growth centers at both ends—one for the stem and one for the roots. To watch the process is to see the magick at work.

A standard seed catalog will show you that there are more varieties of plants available in seed form than you will find in any garden shop or nursery. The seeds will give you several plants at a fraction of the cost of a nursery-grown plant. And every time you grow plants from seed you gain experience and knowledge in the mysteries of nature.

There are a few supplies you will need to get started. You will need a seed tray to hold the starter mix and seeds. These trays are like miniature greenhouses, each with a clear top. Peat pots and plastic cell packs to place inside these trays may also be used. These items are available at any local garden shop or nursery for a few dollars. You can also make do with common household items as well, such as egg cartons, disposable aluminum pans, cut-down milk cartons, or old cake pans. Whatever you use should be 2–3 inches deep. Just make sure to drill drainage holes.

You will need a starter mixture for your seeds. Good commercial mixes are soilless and contain sphagnum peat moss, vermiculite, and perlite. If you wish to mix your own, use equal parts of those three ingredients. It is a very light medium that drains well and promotes healthy root development. Mix the ingredients together, and place the starter mix in a Ziploc plastic bag and add water a little at a time. The mixture should be moist but not soaked. Spread the seed starter mix into the cell packs or directly into the tray. Sow the seeds in the mix. Be sure to read the seed packet for important sowing instructions (you will find information such as light requirements for seed germination and germination times). Loosely cover the tray with the clear cover or with plastic wrap. Be sure to remove the dome or plastic at the first sign of germination, and watch for too much buildup of moisture on the plastic. You don't want to rot the seeds.

Some seeds will need to be stratified before planting. To do so, the seeds must be exposed to temperatures below 32°F

117

because the seed coat contains a germination inhibitor that will be broken down by freezing. One method is to moisten a paper towel. Add the seeds and fold the towel. Place the moistened paper towel with the seeds in a plastic bag and refrigerate or freeze for at least 6 weeks. You may also mix the seed with moistened seed starter, place in a plastic bag, and refrigerate.

If you have sown your seeds directly into flats, transplant the seedlings when they have grown their first set of true leaves. If you wait too long you may damage the stems during the transplanting. Use the "wrong" end of a spoon to prick out the seedlings and transplant them to plastic cells. Fill the cells with potting soil. Poke a well into the center of the cell, and then set in the seedling. Fill in around the plant with a little potting mix.

Be sure to label your seed flats. Use commercial labels sold at plant shops, or make your own out of anything from Popsicle sticks to masking tape. Use indelible ink on your labels.

At some point in your planting, some seeds may fail to germinate. There are several reasons for this.

The seeds may have been planted too deep. The depth of the planting should be twice the thickness of the seed.

The soil may be too wet or too dry. The moisture in the soil needs to be kept even.

Too low a temperature could also cause a failure or delay of germination. The best germination rate is achieved at 70°F (21°C).

Failure of germination may also be due to poor quality seed. Germination rates also decrease the longer the seeds are stored.

To help your seeds germinate at the best rate and time you may wish to use a warming mat. This is a waterproof mat with a raised grid on which to set your flat. These are in most seed catalogs under "Supplies." There are many versions and price ranges for such heaters but the principle remains the same. They raise the temperature 10 to 15 degrees and increase germination rates.

Direct sowing of seeds is worth trying. This is done by preparing the soil in the fall to the requirements of the plant being sowed, and then sowing the seed. Plants that respond well to direct sowing are German chamomile, sage, and borage. These seeds sown in fall will sprout in spring. Be sure to know what the seedlings will look like: You do not want to mistake them for weeds and pull them out!

Be on the watch for the fungal disease known as damping off. This disease will attack seedlings without warning and will lead to collapse of the plant. The stem of the seedling will wither at the soil level while the leaves remain untouched. Dispose of the affected plants. If caught in time, move any remaining plants to an area with better air circulation. To prevent damping off, presoak seeds in water with a couple of crushed cloves of garlic. The fungicidal properties of the garlic will help prevent the disease. You can also make a spray using 1 clove of mashed garlic to 1 quart of water. Strain the garlic pieces, save the liquid, and pour into a spray bottle with the water.

When it is time to plant your seedlings in the garden, you may plant the young seedlings closer and a little deeper than usual to allow them to make better use of the water available in the soil. However, this will make the plants more susceptible to fungal diseases. Some plants require more air circulation around the leaves than others. At the first sign of disease, remove an infected plant.

OTHER METHODS
OF PROPAGATING HERBS

Not all herbs are suited to start from seed. The plants grown from the seed of hybrids and cultivated species, known as cultivars, may not breed true. This means they may not resemble the parent plant. Some hybrids and cultivars have long and difficult germination times. There are other ways to propagate these more difficult plants.

Cuttings are used with woody, shrublike plants such as wormwood, salvia, lavender, and hyssop. In midsummer, cut a green, nonwoody stem just below a node 3–6 inches from the tip of a stem. This type of stem is this year's growth. Use only healthy stems for cuttings. Cut the stem at a 45-degree angle using a sharp knife. Remove all leaves below the first two. Dip the cutting in a rooting hormone. This will help encourage new root growth. Use a light potting mix, such as sand or a peatmoss/vermiculite/perlite mix, to start the cuttings.

Cover the pot loosely with plastic using two sticks to hold the plastic away from the plant. Do not leave the cuttings in direct sunlight. Watch for moisture buildup; too much moisture will rot the cutting. Most herbs will take six weeks to develop sufficient root systems.

Water may also be used as a rooting medium. Place the cutting in a small jar of water. Remember to change the water every day. After rooting in water, plants have a harder time adjusting to growing in soil. You may lose some of your cuttings when transplanting, so take a few extra to begin.

Another form of propagating herbs is called layering. Layering works best with shrubby plants with flexible stems, such as thyme and hyssop. To layer these shrubby plants, bend a stem to the ground. Make a small slit in the tip of the branch and bury it 3–4 inches in the soil. Peg the stem down using a wood peg, a piece of stiff wire bent and sunk into the earth, or a rock set on top, being careful not to crush the stem, of course. When new growth from the pegged area appears, you may sever the new plant from the parent.

Plants have what is called a cambium layer under the bark or surface layer. This cambium layer consists of specialized cells that contain the full genetic codes of the plant and enables the plant to regenerate any part of it that is missing. This allows us to make new plants from cuttings. Root cuttings are taken in the dormant season of the plant. Be sure the roots are young and healthy and are at least 1 inch (2.5 cm) long. You may insert the root cutting vertically for shrubs or trees, or horizontally for perennials.

121

Root division works best with plants with tender stems, such as elecampane, echinacea, and oregano. You may divide this type of perennial plant in spring or fall. If you plan on dividing your herbs in fall, they will need time to settle in before winter, so give them at least six weeks before the first hard frost.

Dig up the plant clump. Some plants—such as chives, monarda, wild geranium, and mountain bluet—may be separated by hand. Just pull the plant apart into smaller clumps and transplant where you wish. Other plants may need more drastic treatment. You may need a sharp knife or shovel to chop the herb into smaller pieces. Just make sure each section has a piece of the crown of the plant. This is where the roots and stems join, and is where new shoots will grow. Make sure each new plant also has a good root system. The smaller the divisions, the more care and attention they will require until they become established. Keep the divisions sufficiently watered until they are well established.

GROWING IN CONTAINERS

Many herbs do well in containers. If you have limited land, or do not want to take on the upkeep of a larger garden, try container gardening. Containers will allow you to grow tender perennials and bring them inside in the autumn. And with containers, you can change the look of your garden simply by moving the pots around.

When growing in containers, you will need a good potting soil. The potting medium needs to be porous and light, as air circulation is very important for the young plants. There are many good commercial mixes on the market from which to choose, but you may wish to mix your own.

To mix your own potting soil you will need the following ingredients:

> A large mixing tub or wheelbarrow,
>   able to hold at least 8 gallons of soil
> 4 gallons of sphagnum peat moss
> 4 gallons of perlite

> 5 tablespoons of limestone
> 3½ tablespoons of superphosphate
> 1 tablespoon of potassium nitrate

Mix the ingredients well. You may wish to add a little magick to the mix. As you combine the ingredients you may recite something like the following:

> With love for life, this soil I mix.
> Plants in pots, their roots will fix.
> Strong and healthy these herbs shall be.
> Plants in pots will grow for me.

I prefer to work with the soil mix in a large wheelbarrow, mixing with my hands. The wheelbarrow has sufficient room for good mixing. You may use any type of large container, such as the plastic tubs found in department stores. It is easier to mix the soil in a tub wider than it is deep. Gloves are optional; some people get clumsy with gloves on and don't mind the feeling of the earth between the fingers and under the fingernails.

Do not use regular garden soil in your containers. Soil right out of the garden may contain weed seeds and soil-borne diseases. It also tends to pack and harden in containers. If you use it for starting seeds, you run the risk of the aforementioned fungal disease damping off, and losing your seedlings. You need to keep the soil light, spongy, and moist for healthy plants.

All your plants will need some basic attention when kept in pots. Keep the soil evenly moist in all containers. Water the plants when the surface soil is dry. As a test, stick a finger into the soil. If it is dry down to an inch below the surface, water the plant. Water your herbs less frequently in winter during their dormant period. Do not let the pots stand in water because it will cause the roots to rot. Use a commercial fertilizer and follow the directions provided on its container. Remove any dead leaves on the plant, and keep the herbs dusted. The dust on the leaves will block the light available to the plant.

Most potted plants will eventually need more room in a larger pot. This is known as potting on. Potting on is done during the growing season and may delay flowering, as the plant will be concentrating on new root growth. There are some plants that prefer confined roots. These plants should have the top 1–2 inches of soil removed from the pot and replaced with fresh soil. These plants should be potted on only when necessary.

Inspect any plants that have been outside when you bring them in for winter. Check for any diseases or insects that might be on the plant. Plants in poor condition can either be destroyed or isolated until the condition is corrected. Pests like aphids or white flies may be controlled by using commercially available sprays or homemade organic substitutes.

Repotting means removing the old soil from the pot. All damaged roots of the plants are removed also. Add fresh soil mix, repot in the same container, and water well.

GROWING IN THE GARDEN

If you decide you want a full-fledged herb garden, you will most likely need to treat your garden soil before planting your herbs. This will get your plants off to a good start and keep them healthier in the long run. Add sand for drainage, and compost and manure for texture. The garden soil should have a crumbly texture. Use a fertilizer with a nitrogen/phosphate/potash ratio of 6:12:12. You may want to add leaf mold or moistened peat moss for water retention. Most herbs prefer a slightly alkaline soil. Add a little lime if your soil is acidic; it will help plants take up the nutrients they need.

A simple way to improve the soil in your garden is to add compost. Composting is a great way to recycle kitchen waste. Vegetable scraps, coffee grounds, ashes from wood fires, and egg shells may be added to your compost heap. You may add paper, too, but avoid any with coloring. Do not add meat, cooked foods, coal or charcoal ashes from your barbecue, house pet litter, or diseased plant material to the heap.

Other materials to add to the compost heap can be found in yard wastes. Leaves, immature weeds that have not gone to seed, and a moderate amount of grass clippings compost well. (Do not add too much grass at one time, as it will inhibit air circulation.) Small branches may be added if they are chopped into pieces.

The ideal size for a compost heap is 1 cubic yard or meter or larger. There are commercial composting bins available at garden centers, but you can also build your own. A simple bin may be made using wooden pallets. All you need is three pallets and some strong wire. Stand the pallets up, forming the letter *U*, and wire them together. The open end will allow you to turn the pile easily.

This material may be left to decompose on its own. This is known as cold or slow composting. There are no additives to hasten the time of decay, and the pile is not turned. The average time of decomposition is about a year. Even then, there will be material that has not totally decomposed. This may be removed and added to a new heap.

Most gardeners prefer what is known as hot composting. The rotting material will actually get hot enough to kill weed seeds. Start this pile with a 3-inch layer of "brown" material such as dried leaves or straw. Add a 3-inch layer of green material, such as kitchen vegetable scraps. Add a little rotted manure. Then add another layer of brown material and continue layering. Turn this pile every 3 weeks or so to add air to the heap. On a cool morning you will see steam rising from the pile. The green matter adds nitrogen to the soil and the brown is rich in carbon. This is food for the microorganisms that will break down the material.

126

Don't be too hasty when pulling weeds. Many weeds found in the garden are also considered herbs and can be used as such. Weeds have been described as herbs growing where they were not planted. Use a field guide to wildflowers to identify a weed. You may decide to leave it where it is or place it in a better spot. Many weeds may have interesting foliage or flowers that can be used medicinally. The Mother provides for her children.

When it is broken down, the compost may then be added to the soil. It may be dug into the garden soil for a new or redug garden, or added as a top dressing for an existing planting.

To help conserve water in the soil, cover the bare spots around the plants with a mulch. Mulch will also keep the soil cooler in summer, prevent soil erosion, and may be used for creating paths. Adding 2–3 inches of mulch will also foster weed control and protect the plant from frost.

A layer of mulch is a great place for small creatures to hide and will attract mice, slugs, and snails. Therefore, one should not mulch expensive shrubs. If you mulch the ground at the shrubs' bases, thinking they will be nice and snug for winter, think again. Come spring, you'll see a sad sight. Most of the shrubs' bark up to the snow line will have been chewed by hungry rodents.

127

HARVESTING YOUR HERBS

Some herbalists consider the thinning of seedlings in spring the first harvest. Continue to harvest early but sparingly in spring and make several major harvests as the herbs come into bloom.

Poisonous and nonpoisonous plants should not be collected or stored together. Do not handle plants when you have open cuts or sores on your hands or skin. This is to prevent direct absorption of chemicals or irritants.

If you are harvesting your herbs for medicinal purposes, start your harvest in early morning, after the sun has evaporated the dew, but before it has dissipated the plants' essential oils. Do not gather more material than you can work with in one morning. The essential oils are most concentrated when the flower buds are just about to blossom. There are of course exceptions: hyssop, oregano, thyme, and the mints are harvested when their blossoms are at their peak, as are yarrow, chamomile, and goldenrod.

Before harvesting, there are two important terms to remember. The term *wood* refers to a large branch or small trunk of a plant that can be cut into manageable pieces. For medicinal purposes, wood is probably the least-used part of a plant. It is more suited to adding flavor and smoking foods.

The term *herbage* refers to the leaves, stalks, and flowers collected together when plants begin to flower. When harvesting your herbs, avoid stalks that are too thick and woody.

When gathering herbs for immediate use, snip at the center of single-stemmed herbs such as basil to encourage bushy side growth. Collect the outermost leaves leaving the crown of the plant to continue growing undisturbed. Trim back perennials by about one-third of their season's growth. For shrubby plants such as rosemary, prune the plant to about half of the year's growth. This trimming will actually strengthen the plant.

Select only the best greens for harvest and avoid any chewed or unhealthy leaves and stalks. Handle the harvest as little as possible to prevent damage. Carry a basket long enough to lay the stalks flat. This type of garden basket is called a trug.

The major harvests of herbs are in July and September. The actual times of collection will vary according to the weather and your location. Traditionally, September is harvest season. Toward the end of the month is the Harvest Moon, the full moon that appears nearest the autumnal equinox. Crops have been harvested by the light of the Harvest Moon for centuries. Annuals can be harvested until the first frost. To allow the plants to harden off and be ready for winter, perennials should be allowed to grow unimpeded for forty to sixty days before the first frost.

To harvest flowers, cut the flower stalks before the blooms are fully open. They will continue to open as they dry. Hang the stalks in a dark place that has freely circulating air. For the harvesting of seed, cut the stalks before seeds begin to loosen from the seed heads. These may begin to ripen between late summer and early fall. Tie up stalks of seed heads, place them in a paper bag, and hang them upside down. The seeds will dry and fall into the bag. Shake loose any remaining seeds.

Collect leaves of herbs when they are young but fully grown. Make sure they are free of garden debris. Dust off any sand or soil, and be sure there are no insects on the plant. When harvesting leaves, always cut the stems; do not just strip

129

off individual leaves. Lay the stems in a single layer so the leaves do not overlap. Turn or stir herbs once or twice during each day until they are dry. Be sure to wait for the leaves and aerial parts to fade and turn brown.

Roots and rhizomes are usually dug up at the end of summer or in early fall. A rhizome is actually part of a stem that is underground, designed by Nature to be a storage organ for the energy the plants need for growth. Hard, woody roots need to dry and be stored in a cool, dry area. The longer the herbs are kept whole, the longer they will maintain their potency. Be sure to shake or brush off soil before storing roots and rhizomes.

Bark is collected in the spring when the flow of sap is at its peak and active plant chemicals are their most potent. To collect the bark, make parallel cuts up and down a branch and lift off small portions of bark. This will allow the plant to heal properly.

> When harvesting the bark of trees or shrubs, do not girdle the branch. It will die. Girdling is the removal of bark in one continuous circle around a branch. The plant will not recover from this type of damage. It is the same damage that mice inflict when they remove the bark of a tree under the snow line in winter.

Collect fruit when it begins to ripen. Ripening will continue after harvesting. Remove the seeds from mature fruit if you wish. Remove any fleshy covering from the seeds to prevent spoilage. Store the seeds in the refrigerator until you are ready to plant.

Dry herbs may be substituted for fresh herbs in cooking and vice versa. Fresh plant material contains much more water and so is less potent than when it is in dried form. When substituting dry herbs for fresh, use half the suggested amount. When substituting fresh for dried, double the amount.

It is always important to thank the Goddess and the Earth for providing for you, her daughters and sons. Recite a few words or a chant similar to the following as you harvest the plants you have nurtured:

131

Herbs for cooking and herbs for health.
I thank the herbs for their given wealth.
I thank the Earth for providing for me.
I thank the Goddess. So mote it be.

Many trees are considered sacred, and their branches are often collected by Wiccans, for use as wands, staffs, and stangs. A stang is a forked staff that is used by some traditions to hold banners or to mark the quarters. The height of a staff or stang should be no higher than your shoulder.

Sacred trees include alder, apple, birch, hawthorn, holly, oak, and poplar. Each has its own magickal associations that may be used in different ritual work.

TYPES OF HERBAL PREPARATIONS

Before you start any preparation, be sure you know the herbs you are using and what effect they will have on your body. Do not use any preparation, especially if you are pregnant, without consulting a health-care professional. Do not use any herbs for more than four to six weeks.

> The strength of any herbal preparation will vary from garden to garden and plant to plant. Many factors affect the potency of your herbal preparations (e.g., sunlight, soil, drying and storing, and preparation method).

Decoctions

A decoction is made from herbs that have been simmered in water. This is the best method for drawing the healing elements from tough plant parts such as bark, roots, stems, berries, and heavy leaves.

To make a decoction, use 1 ounce of dried herbs to 1 pint of boiling water. Then keep water just below boiling for about thirty minutes and let herbs simmer. Note that simmering may take up to an hour, depending on the toughness of the plant parts.

Decoctions should always be strained while hot, so that the matter that separates on cooling can be mixed back into the fluid by shaking when the remedy is used. Use glass; ceramic or earthenware pots; or clean, unbroken enameled cast iron. Do not use plain cast iron with astringent plants. Make fresh decoctions daily. Cover and store unused portions in the refrigerator.

A teacup-size dose is the standard for decoction. Take this dose three times a day. The decoction may be cold or reheated. Reduce the dosage for the elderly and children.

> Use the crushed seeds of fennel *(Foeniculum vulgare)* in a decoction for indigestion with flatulence, or irritable bowel syndrome. Use ½ teaspoon crushed seed to 1 cup boiling water. Simmer for twenty to thirty minutes, and strain. Drink 3 to 4 cups of this decoction per day.

133

Electuary

When powders are mixed with syrup, honey, brown sugar, or glycerin to produce a more pleasant taste or to make them easier to use internally, they are called electuaries. These are rarely prepared in advance, but are made fresh as needed. Different substances need different proportions of syrup. Light vegetable powders usually require twice their weight, gum resins two-thirds their weight, mineral substances about half their weight. If an electuary is made up in advance and it hardens, add more syrup. If it swells up and emits gas, merely beat it in a mortar.

The dosage depends on the herb and the illness.

Extracts (Tinctures)

Extracts—also known as tinctures—are solid substances resulting from the evaporation of the solution of vegetable principles. The extract is obtained in three ways: by expressing the juice of fresh plants, by using a solvent such as alcohol, or simmering a plant tea and reducing it to a thickened state. The last method involves simmering a plant repeatedly until most of the water has evaporated, making a decoction. This leaves you with a distillation of the most active principles in the plant. Add ¼ teaspoon of alcohol (brandy, gin, or vodka will do), glycerin, or tincture of benzoin to preserve the extract.

134

Carrots are a great source of vitamin A, in the form of carotene, a substance thought to help fight cancer. Boil ¾ cup of water. Grate 1 pound of carrots and their leaves and add to the boiling water. Cook until very thick.

Fomentations

A fomentation is a strong herbal tea in which a clean cloth is dipped. The cloth can be filled with herbs. The moist cloth is then applied directly to the affected body part. Wrap the body part. Repeat as required.

Infusions

An infusion may be revitalizing or relaxing. It is similar to a tea. The herbs for an infusion may be dried or fresh.

To make a hot infusion, heat water. Do not bring it to a full boil, as you may lose volatile oils in the steam. Add 1 teaspoon of the dried herb, or 1 tablespoon fresh herb, to the water. Cover and let steep for nine to thirteen minutes. Strain and cool the liquid. Infusions are sipped as teas, added to a bath, and used to anoint the body. Powdered bark, root, seeds, resin and bruised nuts, and buds may be used in hot infusions. You may use a single herb, known as a simple, or a combination of herbs.

To make a cold infusion, steep the herb in cold water or cold milk for several hours. These wet, mashed herbs can be used internally as a tea or as poultices on the body.

A teacup-size dose is the standard for an infusion. Take this dose three times a day. The infusion may be cold or reheated. Reduce the dosage for the elderly and children.

135

> Drink an infusion of basil *(Ocimum basilicum)* in combination with motherwort just after childbirth. This combination of herbs helps expel the placenta.

Oils

Infused oils are used externally as massage oils, creams, and ointments. The active plant chemicals are extracted using an oil such as sunflower oil. Oils will last up to a year if kept in a cool, dark place. There are two methods of preparing an infused oil: cold infusion and hot infusion.

For cold infusion, pick your own fresh herbs or purchase dried herbs from a reputable source. Fill a large jar with the herb and pour in your favorite monounsaturated or polyunsaturated oil, adding enough oil to cover the herb. Close the jar tightly. Label it and place it in a sunny location for several weeks. Strain out the herb by pouring the liquid through a piece of cheesecloth into an empty jar. Hold the cheesecloth over the opening of the jar containing the herbs and secure with a rubber band. Invert the jar and pour the infused oil through the cheesecloth. Before discarding the herbs, squeeze all the oil out of them. Repeat the entire procedure. Repack a clean jar with more of the same herb. Add the infused oil, plus enough additional oil to cover the herbs. Store again in sunlight. Strain again through cheesecloth. Pour the oil into a labeled jar and store until needed. Do not take essential oils internally.

To alleviate the pain of a toothache, put 1 to 2 drops of the essential oil of nutmeg (*Myristica fragrans*) on a cotton swab. Apply the oil to the gums on the affected area. Then make an appointment to see your dentist as soon as possible.

To make a hot infused oil you will need a double boiler or a glass bowl over a pan of hot water. Put the oil into the bowl and add the herb. Heat the oil and herbs gently for three hours. Strain the liquid into a clean, airtight jar.

> Use the essential oil of Saint-John's-wort *(Hypericum perforatum)* in combination with lavender oil for burns, or yarrow for inflammation of joints.

137

Ointments

An ointment is a soothing, healing, slightly oily or fatty substance into which the essence of a healing herb has been dissolved by heating the fat or oil with the herb until the plant loses its normal colors. The plant material is then removed by straining, and beeswax is added as a hardener. You may wish to add a few drops of a tincture of benzoin, poplar bud tincture, or glycerin as a preservative. If you make ointments in small batches and keep them tightly closed with paraffin wax, they should not decompose.

The traditional folk, herbal, and pharmaceutical base for ointments is pork lard. The lard is purified by simmering and straining. It is said to have healing abilities even without the addition of herbs, but so do a lot of fats and oils. It is also said to have great drawing power.

Purified, liquefied, anhydrous lanolin is also used as a base for ointments. Lanolin is the substance washed from the wool of sheep. It comes in many levels of purity, so the results will vary depending on the product. This oil is the closest to human skin oil. Almond oil, cocoa butter, wheat germ, and vitamin E are all neutral bases that may be used for ointments.

> Use an ointment made with Roman chamomile (*Chamaemelum nobile*) to soothe the itch of insect bites, eczema, and irritation around the anus and vulva.

All ointments must contain one substance that will thicken the final product. Lanolin is used as a thickener, as is cocoa butter. Both are nonsticky and mix well with most other oils. Other useful thickeners are glycerin, honey, or liquid lecithin, but they tend to be sticky. Also, various powdered resins and gums will swell and thicken when they are first soaked in cold water. Agar-agar and Irish moss are seaweed thickeners. Thickeners are simmered in gently boiling water and added to preparations.

While any of the above thickeners will help swell a preparation and keep it emulsified, you will still need some wax to harden a homemade cream or ointment. Beeswax is perfect, although expensive. It may be combined with paraffin wax to reduce the cost.

Chickweed *(Stellaria media)* makes a slight astringent and soothing ointment. Use chickweed ointment for easing irritation and healing wounds.

Poultices

A poultice is made with raw or mashed herbs applied directly to the body, or applied wet directly to the body, or encased in a clean cloth and then applied. Poultices are used to heal bruises and putrid sores, to soothe abrasions, or to withdraw toxins from an area. Cold poultices (and compresses) are used to withdraw the heat from an inflamed area and soothe skin irritations. Use a hot poultice or compress to relax spasms and for some pains.

To make a poultice, use fresh or dried herbs that have been soaked in boiling water until soft. You will need enough of the herb to cover the affected part. You may use the herb as it is, or mix it with slippery elm powder to make the poultice stick together. Place the poultice on the affected area and then wrap the body part and the herbs with a clean cloth. Repeat every two to four hours.

Plantain *(Plantago major)* may be used for bee stings, slowly healing wounds, and poison ivy. Mash fresh plantain leaves and apply them directly to the affected area. Repeat as necessary.

139

Syrups

Medicinal syrups are formed when sugar is added to vegetable infusions and decoctions. Sometimes tinctures are combined with sugar and gently heated, or exposed to the sun until the alcohol is evaporated. The syrup is then prepared with the sugar and water. Refined sugar makes a clearer and better-flavored syrup, but you may use unrefined sugar or honey. Any simple syrup can be preserved by substituting glycerin for a certain portion of the syrup. Always make syrups in small quantities, as they can spoil quickly.

> For a soothing expectorant for colds and bronchitis, make a syrup from a decoction of licorice (*Glycyrrhiza glabra*).

To make an herbal syrup, add 2 ounces of dried herb with 1 quart of water in a large pot. Boil down and reduce to 1 pint, then add 1 to 2 tablespoons of honey. If you want to use fresh fruit, leaves, or roots in syrups, you should double the amount of herbs. Store in refrigerator for up to a month. Honey-based syrups are a simple and effective way to preserve healing qualities of herbs. Syrups can soothe sore throats and provide some relief from coughs.

Teas

Homemade herbal teas are much more potent than the store-bought teas. Their flavor can be quite strong and sometimes unpleasant. To make a tea, boil 1 pint of water. Add 1 ounce of dried herb tops (leaves, flowers, or stems) and steep for three to five minutes. Teas are essentially infusions but are consumed as a beverage.

For a good-tasting tea that stimulates and aids digestion, try a tea made from catnip *(Nepeta cataria)*. Catnip tea is rich in vitamin C and is a soothing drink before bedtime.

141

Tinctures

Tinctures are solutions of medicinal substances in alcohol or diluted alcohol. The active ingredients are extracted by the alcohol, which also serves as a preservative. Do not use denatured, rubbing, or industrial alcohol to make your tinctures. A tincture can be stored up to two years.

To make a tincture, grind plant parts with a mortar and pestle (or a blender). Add just enough high-quality vodka, whiskey, or grain alcohol to cover the herbs. Let sit for twenty-one days, then add a small quantity of glycerin (about 2 tablespoons per pint) and about 10 percent volume of spring water. Strain and store in airtight amber-colored glass.

Fumitory *(Fumaria officinalis)* is used as a tincture for liver and gallbladder problems. You will find this plant growing in almost any garden as a "weed." Diarrhea and stomachache will result if this herb is used in excess.

For a stronger tincture, place powdered or cut herbs in a cone-shaped piece of parchment paper. Pass alcohol repeatedly through the herb. Catch the drippings in a glass jar. You may use it on the first pass through, but the more you repeat the process, the stronger the tincture will be. It is acceptable to dilute any alcohol tincture with water. Add 4 ounces of water and 1 teaspoon of glycerin for every pint of alcohol. The glycerin is optional; it is an additional preservative.

A standard dose of a tincture is 5 milliliters diluted in a small amount of warm water. Take the tincture three or four times a day, with a little sugar or honey to taste.

Nonalcoholic Tincture

If you are pregnant, avoid alcohol tinctures. There is an alternate way to prepare a tincture. If you wish to evaporate the alcohol, add the tincture dose to a cup of water, and then add ⅛ to ¼ teaspoon of boiling water. The boiling water will evaporate the alcohol. Some herbs can be steeped in milk to make a milk tincture. Strain out the herbs, and store in a labeled jar in the refrigerator.

Amaranth *(Amaranthus hypochondriacus)* has been used for diarrhea and excessive menstrual bleeding. Use an amaranth tincture in a dose of ½ to 1 teaspoon.

Vinegars

Herbs that are soluble in alcohol are usually soluble in vinegar, and are useful for salad vinegars, cosmetic vinegars, some liniments, and preventive washes.

To make an herbal vinegar, use 1 cup of fresh herbs to 1 quart of vinegar. You may choose to use cider vinegar, red wine vinegar, or white wine vinegar. Always look for an acid level of 8 percent or higher.

Harvest the herb after the morning dew has dried. Wash if necessary, then pat dry. A milder herb vinegar will be produced by using herbs in flower. Choose a tall, clean glass bottle, such as a wine or olive oil bottle. Place herbs into the bottle, add the vinegar to cover the herbs, and then cork the bottle. Find a cool, dark place to let the vinegar stand for at least three to four weeks. Check the bottles after a couple of days. You may need to add more vinegar to recover the herbs. After the infusion period, you may seal the bottles by dipping the corked bottle top in melted wax. The herbal vinegar should be used within a year.

Herbal vinegars make wonderful gifts. Beautiful bottles are available at your local kitchen-supply store. Use these vinegars in salads, steamed veggies, or in sauces. Paste a label on the bottle with the type of vinegar and expiration date.

Washes and Waters

Washes, also known as waters, are actually diluted infusions or diluted tinctures. They are used to bathe wounds, sores, and other skin afflictions. To use, soak a cotton ball in the wash. Bathe the area from the center outward.

Use a decoction of oats *(Avena sativa)* as a wash for skin conditions. Apply as necessary.

Conclusion

When I am in the garden I feel a connection with the Earth. Nothing matters other than the garden. I work the soil, transplant seedlings, or decide I want to move things around. I sit in front of a new section of the garden in the backyard and envision what I hope to accomplish with it. Should I move a clump of the motherwort from the nursery bed to this new section or to the front garden for vertical interest? Is that rue flourishing here, or should I move it to a better spot? The feverfew is getting leggy and needs more sun.

I don't plan the garden on paper, just in my head. A professional landscape gardener, which I am not, would cringe at the thought. I believe I learn to build a better garden simply by mixing the textures and colors of the foliage and flowers. When I find a combination that doesn't work, I will move it. I have fun moving the plants, and as they are hardy perennials, they don't seem to mind too much, as long as I give them plenty of time before winter to adjust.

No thoughts of my day job. No thoughts of a negative kind, except maybe when I find that the grasshoppers have chewed the buds off the plants! It is as if all the negative energy I may emit is pulled into the soil and converted into positive energy. I nurture the Earth as the Earth nurtures and gives food and healing plants to us all. I tend to my small gardens around the house and feel the beauty of what nature is. I feel the energy of the Earth, as anyone in a garden can. You can feel it in a large, rambling country estate garden, and you can feel it in a small patch of a garden near an urban back door.

Reverence for all life and the Earth on which we live— that is what we are about. We are all connected, Wiccan and non-Wiccan, animals and plants. All are connected to the Earth and to each other. As humans, we have the future of this world in our hands. We must take care and determine our destiny, and the destiny of other creatures, very carefully.

—DEBBIE MICHAUD, A.K.A. GREYWING

146

Tools for the Herbalist

Most of the supplies you will use to make herbal preparations can be found in any kitchenware shop or hardware store.

Blender A blender is not a necessity but it can make things a little easier. It also ensures that the herb is cut to a consistent size.

Cheesecloth You will need cheesecloth for straining preparations such as decoctions and infusions. You can buy it at your local grocery store.

Cutting board These now come in a variety of materials. Try one made of stone, glass, ceramic, or hard plastic.

Funnels Find some funnels in different sizes for the jars you have. Have two sets on hand. Use one for edible and the other for nonedible preparations.

Jars Dark glass is preferred for storing herbal preparations as it helps keep them safe from light damage and protects the potency of the herbs.

Knives Make sure your knives are sharp. Steel blades are preferable.

Labels Be sure to label all your jars after filling them. You may use mailing labels, file folder labels, or any labels you have on hand. Mark the content and the date it was bottled in indelible ink.

Measuring cups and spoons Keep two sets of each on hand: one for edible, the other for inedible products.

Mortar and pestle A mortar and pestle are not essential if you have a blender, but they are fun for grinding herbs. You may find, after buying your first, that you develop an incredible urge to collect them. They are made of various materials—glass, marble, ceramic, wood—and are all quite beautiful in their own way.

Pots and pans Use enamel, glass, or stainless steel pots and pans. Do not use aluminum as it will leach into your product. Keep two sets: one for inedible products only.

Pruning scissors Keep your pruners sharp for harvesting. Clean and dry them after use. Wiccans may use their boline, if they have one, to harvest for healing or magick.

Screening Window screens, available in various sizes at your local hardware store, will be used for drying herbs.

Wax Wax is used to seal the jars filled with your preparations.

Terms You May Find on Your Path

The following is a list of terms you will come across on your journey. This list is by no means complete. Other terms are scattered through the pages of this book as needed, and may not be duplicated here.

Akashic Records   A giant database that can be accessed by the mind through Universal connections. This database holds information on past lives and healing, among other things.

Amulet   An object of protection that has been ritually charged. These items deflect negative energies, including thoughts, and are usually worn around the neck. An amulet can be made of anything you feel is appropriate: feathers, shells, beads, stones, etc.

Ankh   Known as the Egyptian Cross of Life or the Key of the Nile. The marriage of the Goddess and the God was to have taken place at the source of the river. The ankh is a sexual symbol, with a female oval and a male cross. It is thought of as a universal life charm. The word *life* is the translation of the hieroglyphic.

Astral   The astral plane is considered another dimension of reality. It is also known by the Australian Aboriginal name of Dreamtime. The traveler's consciousness leaves the body and experiences the environment from above.

Bane   From the Old English *bana*, meaning bad, evil, or destructive.

Bind   To use magick to restrain someone or something. Binding spells are used for this purpose.

"Blessed Be"   This phrase is common in Wicca, to remind us of the spiritual connection we all share. It is used as a greeting and a good-bye.

Blood of the Moon   The menstrual cycle. This is a very powerful time for women. If the woman acknowledges the strength she holds within, she is more powerful at this time than any other.

Chakras   These are seven major energy sites found on the human body. Each is associated with a color: the Crown chakra's associated color is white; the Forehead (third eye), purple; the Throat, blue; the Chest, pink or green; the Navel, yellow; the Abdomen, orange; and the Groin, red.

Cone of Power   This is energy that has been raised and focused for a specific purpose, whether solitary or in a coven.

Once raised, the power is sent out into the Universe to act for that purpose.

Consecration Dedication to a sacred purpose and use.

Dedication The act of dedicating oneself to learning the way of the chosen path. The traditional duration is a year and a day of learning.

Deosil A clockwise movement, like that of the sun.

Drawing Down the Moon A full-moon ritual used to empower the witch performing the ritual and unite her essence with the Goddess. It is usually performed with a coven.

Druid From the Old Irish *drui* (there are many variations on the name, such as *dryads* and *druidai*). The followers of Druidism consider the oak to be a sacred tree. Druidism is attacked by the Church not only for its paganism but also because women are allowed to participate. Druid traditions are kept alive by passing down songs and ballads.

151

Gaea The Earth was made in the image of Gaea. This is the name of the Mother Earth goddess of the Greeks. She was the universal mother of creation. She gave birth to the Titans, the first humans. Mother Earth created mountains, rivers, and seas. Gaea was also respected as a prophetess.

Grimoire Ceremonial magicians' version of the Book of Shadows. It contains spells and recipes of "High Magick."

Handfasting A Pagan or Wiccan marriage ceremony, performed by a priestess.

Invoke   Is to cause to appear, usually for support.

Matriarchy   A line of descent that is traceable though the women's side of the family. It is used to affirm a time when power and rule passed down from mother to daughter.

Name, or Craft Name   It is a common practice to choose a name for Craft purposes, often through meditation. Names of deities and characters of myths and legends are popular. Some trads have you choose a craft name that will be used in the group and one that is known only to you. There are books on the market to help you choose one.

Pantheon   This is a collection or group of Gods and Goddesses in a particular mythic or religious structure. For example, the Greek pantheon contains Selene the Moon Goddess, and Aphrodite, the Goddess of love. Wiccans are free to choose which god or goddess to work with and may even mix pantheons.

Scrying   Using a mirror, crystal ball, water, or other reflective tools for divination. These tools are focal points for the mind to see images it can interpret.

Skyclad   Rituals performed in the nude. Some Wiccans think it is easier to raise power and to send energy that is raised out of the body if the worker is nude.

Spiral   A sacred, ancient symbol. It is connected to the cycle of death and rebirth. Many folk dances trace a spiral when performed.

Virgin   Independence, especially from men. The woman who is a virgin is her own person.

Visualization   A technique to see in your mind what you wish. It is used in spell work and healing. Wishing is not enough; you have to see it.

Watchtowers and Watchers   It is taught in some systems of magick that there are two sets of portals in a magick circle. Think of a circle within a circle. The inner circle contains Portals of the Elementals at the East, South, West, and North. The outer circle contains the Portals of the Watchers, also known as Astral Portals. The space between the two circles is known as "The World Between the Worlds." Some are taught that this dimension must exist for ritual or magickal energies to flow between the Worlds. The Elemental Portals represent the point of access to the Elemental Plane which exists between the Physical and Nonphysical, or Astral, Dimensions. The Elemental Rulers guard the Portals between this World and the Astral.

153

   The Watchers are said to guard the direct access to the Astral Plane. Each Watcher has its own Watchtower. It is taught they have the power to cancel your magick. The concept of the Watchers is based in the magickal system known as Enochian Magick.

Widdershins   The opposite of deosil: a counterclockwise movement against the sun.

BIBLIOGRAPHY

Adler, Margot. *Drawing Down the Moon* (rev. ed.). Boston: Beacon Press, 1986.

Bannatyne, Lesley Prate. *Halloween: An American Holiday, An American History*. Gretna, La.: Pelican Publishing, 1998.

Beyerl, Paul. *The Master Book of Herbalism*. Custer, Wa.: Phoenix Publishing Inc., 1984.

Blamires, Steve. *Glamoury, Magic of the Celtic Green World*. St. Paul, Minn.: Llewellyn Publications, 1995.

Bremness, Lesley. *Herbs*. New York: Readers Digest Association, 1990.

Brickell, Christopher. *The American Horticultural Society Encyclopedia of Gardening*. London: Dorling Kindersley, 1993.

Brueton, Diana. *The Moon: Myth, Magic and Fact*. New York: Barnes and Noble Inc., 1998.

Bubel, Nancy. *The New Seed-Starters Handbook*. Emmaus, Penn.: Rodale Press, 1988.

Christ, Carol P. *Rebirth of the Goddess*. Reading, Mass.: Addison-Wesley, 1997.

Conway, D. J. *Maiden, Mother, Crone*. St. Paul, Minn.: Llewellyn Publications, 1995.

Damrosch, Barbara. *The Garden Primer*. New York: Workman Publishing, 1988.

Eisler, Riane. *The Chalice & The Blade*. San Francisco: HarperCollins, 1988.

Gilbertie, Sal. *Kitchen Herbs*. New York: Bantam, 1988.

Grieve, Mrs. M. *A Modern Herbal*. vols. 1 and 2. New York: Dover Publications, 1982.

Harvey, Graham, and Charlotte Hardman. *Paganism Today*. London: Thorsons, 1995.

Hoffman, David. *The Herbal Handbook: A User's Guide to Medical Herbalism*. Rochester, Vt.: Healing Arts Press, 1987.

Hufton, Olwin. *The Prospect Before Her: A History of Women in Western Europe 1500–1800*. New York: Vintage Books, 1995.

Husain, Sharukh. *The Goddess*. New York: Little, Brown, 1997.

Hutchens, Alma R. *Indian Herbalogy of North America*. Boston: Shambhala Publications, 1991.

Kowalchik, Claire (ed.). *Rodale's Illustrated Encyclopedia of Herbs*. Emmaus, Penn.: Rodale Press, 1987.

Kruger, Anna. *An Illustrated Guide to Herbs: Their Medicine and Magick*. London: Parkgate Books, 1997.

Lathrop, Norma Jean. *Herbs: How to Select, Grow and Enjoy*. Los Angeles: HP Books, 1981.

Lust, John. *The Herb Book*. New York: Bantam, 1974.

McArthur, Margie. *Wisdom of the Elements*. Freedom, Calif.: The Crossing Press, 1998.

McGuffin, Michael (ed.). *American Herbal Products Association's Botanical Safety Handbook*. Boca Raton, Fla.: CRC Press, 1997.

Moorey, Teresa. *A Beginner's Guide to Witchcraft*. London: Hodder & Stoughton, 1996.

Ody, Penelope. *The Complete Medicinal Herbal*. London: Dorling Kindersley, 1993.

Purkiss, Diane. *The Witch in History*. New York: Routledge, 1996.

PDR for Herbal Medicines. Montvale, N.J.: Medical Economics Company, 1998.

Radford, E. and M.A. Radford. *The Encyclopedia of Superstitions*. Oxford, England: Helicon Publishing Ltd., 1995.

Stein, Diane. *All Women Are Healers*. Freedom, Calif.: Crossing Press, 1990.

Stein, Diane. *The Women's Book of Healing*. St. Paul, Minn.: Llewellyn Publications, 1994.

Streep, Peg. *Altars Made Easy*. San Francisco: HarperCollins, 1997.

Valiente, Doreen. *The Rebirth of Witchcraft*. Custer, Wa.: Phoenix Publishing Inc., 1989.

Walker, Barbara. *The Woman's Dictionary of Symbols and Sacred Objects*. San Francisco: HarperCollins, 1988.

Walker, Barbara. *The Women's Encyclopedia of Myths and Secrets*. Edison, N.J.: Castle Books, 1983.

Weiss, Gaea, and Shandor Weiss. *Growing & Using The Healing Herbs*. New York: Wings Books, 1992.

INDEX

('b' indicates boxed material; 't' indicates a table)

165